WIPEOUTS!

There are countless ways to put down your fellowman, but none is more satisfying than the clever verbal crusher. A witty retort can dispose of a bore and leave a bully speechless, helpless, and destroyed.

Here is an anthology of some of the world's best squelches.

W9-AAJ-042

WIPEOUTS!
is an original Pocket Book edition.

Also by Al Boliska

The Mahareeshi Says . . .
The World's Worst Jokes

Published by Pocket Books

**Are there paperbound books you want
but cannot find in your retail stores?**

WIPEOUTS!

AL BOLISKA

PUBLISHED BY POCKET BOOKS NEW YORK

WIPEOUTS!

A *Pocket Book* edition

1st printing............May, 1969

This original *Pocket Book* edition is printed from
brand-new plates made from newly set, clear, easy-to-read type.
Pocket Book editions are published by Pocket Books, a division of
Simon & Schuster, Inc., 630 Fifth Avenue, New York, N.Y. 10020.
Trademarks registered in the United States and other countries.

L

Standard Book Number: 671-55097-7.

FOR

BEVERLEY

Introduction

There are countless ways to put down your fellowman:

You can pound him into the ground with a heavy, blunt instrument.

You can fink on him

You can ambush him.

You can harass him from his flanks.

You can hang, shoot, stab, flog, strangle, drown, or burn him.

But none of these is so satisfying as a successful verbal squelch. Not JUST a tongue-lashing, but an honest-to-God wipeout that leaves a man speechless, helpless, and destroyed.

If it is deserved, and happens before his fellows, so much the better. If it's funny . . . great!

What qualifies as a wipeout? It must not be an overwhelming barrage of obscenities. That would leave most civilized adversaries speechless all right, but it's not what we're after.

To be able to flatten a man twice your size with one lightning blow of your magic mouth . . . there's the joy! To be clever. To have the last word. To turn a man against himself. To shoot him with his own bullets. To be funny. To play with words. To use them swiftly and devastatingly. And if the victim is one deserving of an oral crush, so much greater the ecstasy of the victor.

Here follows an anthology of some of the world's great wipeouts.

". . . Although we feel you have an excellent idea here, unfortunately. . . ."

Most editors of magazines and books will make an acknowledgment of a manuscript quite promptly, returning it with some indication of interest even to the point of making some personal comment about the writer's work. There are times, however, when the submission is so unforgivably inferior that even the kindliest editor will not resist the temptation to wipe out.

The editor of a large New York publishing house returned one weighty manuscript with the comment:

"I am returning this paper. Someone wrote on it."

One would-be novelist attached a note to his work asking:

"Do you think I should put more fire into my stories?"

The editor returned the manuscript with the observation:

"No, I think the opposite."

A similar story has the poet offering a series to a national magazine with the comment:

"Please let me know if you like these and plan to use them. I have other irons in the fire."

His work was returned by the next post with the editor's remark:

"Remove irons and insert poems."

On a trans-Atlantic passage, Sinclair Lewis intently watched an old lady reading his latest novel. It was one which had caused much discussion, containing one or two passages that tended to shock with their candid discourse on bedroom adventure.

By the number of pages she had apparently read, it was evident that she was about to come to the first of these.

Presently, before his very eyes, Lewis watched the little lady get up, walk to the rail, and fling the book far out into the sea.

Rejection slip: "Get your tripewriter fixed."

A would-be novelist burst into the office of the publisher who had turned down his manuscript.

"You turned this down," he screamed. "Yet you didn't read it all. I glued together several pages in the book just to trick you. I glued together pages 16 and 17, 22 and 23, and 58 and 59. You read just a tiny part of it. . . . Is that honest?"

"Sir," said the editor, "when my wife serves me an absolutely horrible breakfast, I don't have to eat the whole thing to realize how bad it is."

"Darling, I read your new book yesterday. I loved it. Who wrote it for you?"

"I'm glad you liked it. Who read it to you?"

3

"In conclusion, let me say, Renard's latest book has one major thing wrong with it. The covers are too far apart."

July 21, 1931

Dear Mr. Rosengren:

I am in receipt of Lady Holland's *Memoirs* and you were certainly right in bestowing your popular-priced sympathy on me. I have started to wade through the first volume, and it reads like the diary of a lame nun who had served forty years of solitary confinement for ogling a gouty bishop in a moment of post-puberty weakness. Ere it is finished, I know that a recent endowment policy will expire which is the only thing I have to which I can look forward.

Fred Allen

Frank Case, manager of New York's Algonquin Hotel in the 1920's when it was a favorite stopping place for the literati of the day, had a fairly universal taste in reading, but he could not bear the horrors of William Faulkner's books.

He met Faulkner in the hotel lobby one day. "How are you?" he asked the great man.

"Not too well," replied Faulkner. "I've had an upset stomach lately."

"Something you wrote, no doubt," quipped Case.

Dorothy Parker, who signed her book reviews "Constant Reader," reviewed one of A. A. Milne's saccharine efforts with:

". . . and at this point, Tonstant Weader fwowed up."

4

"... critics are legless men who teach running. ..."
—CHANNING POLLOCK

Critics, I sometimes think, become critics so they can savor the great joy of squelching people daily.

A young playwright gave a special invitation to a highly regarded critic in New York to attend his off-Broadway epic. The critic came to the play, but slept through all of it.

After the play was over, the young playwright was enraged. He dashed out and shook the critic awake and demanded:

"You ass! You pompous old man! How could you sleep when you knew how much I wanted your opinion?"

The old veteran rubbed his eyes, looked up at the playwright, and murmured:

"Young man, sleep IS an opinion."

A critic once reviewed a concert by an amateur group this way:

"Last night at Massey Hall Auditorium, the Viceroy University Orchestra played Beethoven.

"Beethoven lost."

It was the young playwright's first play on Broadway. Opening night had come and gone. Now, the agony of waiting for the reviews in the morning papers.

He frantically searched the theater pages, but no mention of his opening anywhere! He got on the phone, called up one of the more important gods of the theater, and demanded:

"Why didn't you mention my play? You were there, weren't you?"

"Yes, I was there."

"Well, why didn't you write about it?"

"Frankly, I didn't know how to spell YECCH!"

FIRST KNIFERS

". . . Let me sum up this motion picture by saying, I've seen better film on teeth."

John Mason Brown:
"Tallulah Bankhead barged down the Nile as Cleopatra last night . . . and sank."

George S. Kaufman on a Broadway personality:
"He's the most painsgiving director in the New York theater."

Dorothy Parker's famous line on Katherine Hepburn's performance:
"Katherine Hepburn, in *The Lake,* runs the gamut of emotions from A to B."

". . . Let me just say, I've seen more excitement at the opening of an umbrella."

"And as expected, the play at the Orpheum had a happy ending. When it ended at 12:30 this morning, 1,400 weary first nighters were very happy."

"The director assures me this film was shot in France . . . here, too."

Brooks Atkinson:
"When Mr. Wilbur calls his play *Halfway to Hell*, he underestimates the distance."

Christopher Fry on the performance of a certain actor in one of his plays:
"His pauses are no longer pregnant—they're in labor."

Eugene Field in the *Boston Globe* on *King Lear:*
"He played the king as though someone else held the ace."

Hedda Hopper on a show:
"For the first time in my life, I envied my feet. They were asleep."

". . . Her singing was mutiny on the High C's."

". . . And the least you can say for it is, the play started at 8:30 sharp and ended at 10 o'clock dull."

Rebecca West, reporting on an exhibition of nude paintings by D. H. Lawrence, gave the whole show one line:
"Mr. Lawrence has very pink friends."

Sid Ziff, in Los Angeles, summed up a book review with:
"It's not a book to be lightly thrown aside. It should be thrown with great force."

George S. Kaufman, when he was drama editor of *The New York Times,* reviewed a play with:
"I was underwhelmed!"

"Even at intermission there was a long lineup last night at the Palace Theater. A long lineup of people trying to leave."

A New York critic once observed:

"Sidney Blackmer has been accused of being a very good actor. By his performance in last night's drama he was tried and acquitted."

"I saw the show at a disadvantage. The curtain was up."

"It's the kind of show that starts at 8 sharp. After two hours you look at your watch and it's twenty after eight."

Robert Benchley once made this observation about the long-running play *Abie's Irish Rose:*

"See Hebrews 13:8."

This sent readers scurrying for their Bibles to find that Hebrews 13:8 reads: JESUS CHRIST THE SAME YESTERDAY, AND TODAY, AND TOMORROW.

Dorothy Parker's review on Channing Pollock's *The House Beautiful:*

". . . *The House Beautiful,*" she wrote, "is the play lousy."

". . . Say what you have to say and the first time you come to a sentence with a grammatical ending, sit down!"
—WINSTON CHURCHILL

Men who do a lot of public speaking never really relax with it. They show signs of nervousness even after years of addressing large audiences. That little nervousness you detect is the outward evidence of an internal panic. You never know when one of your enemies is out there somewhere in that audience . . . waiting for the right moment to destroy you in front of a thousand people.

Quote Magazine reports a lovely story about a speaker who had been at the lectern for about two hours. During his long talk, he suffered many interruptions from a chap in the balcony who kept yelling:

"Louder! Louder!" After about the fifth interruption, a gentleman in the first row stood up, looked back, and asked:

"What's the matter my friend, can't you hear?"

"No, I can't hear," came the answer from the balcony.

"Well, then, thank God, and shut up!"

How would you like to continue your talk after that?

Most professional public speakers and lecturers will tell you the best way to immediately get your audience's attention is to open your talk with a startling statement, and then wait for your shocker to sink in . . . .

How horrible to be shot down twenty seconds after you open.

Herb Caen, in the *San Francisco Chronicle,* tells about San Francisco Chapter Three of the California State Employees Association, gathered at the Red Chimney in Stonestown, who heard a speaker ask, while discussing crime:

"Do you know that in New York City, a woman is raped every four and a half hours?"

The stunned silence was broken by Chapter President Lou Tripodi, who ventured:

"She must be the happiest woman in the world."

Professor in lecture hall to inattentive audience:

"Ladies and gentlemen, there are about a thousand people who know as much, or more, about this subject than I do. However, as I look around, I can see that none of them are here tonight, so may I please have your undivided attention?"

A speaker was asked if he would accept a check for his services and then make a present of it to a special fund the organization had started.

"Certainly," agreed our benevolent friend. "What is the fund for?"

"To enable us to get better speakers next year."

Seated next to our victim at a UN dinner was an Oriental fellow dressed in the robes of one of the far-eastern countries.

Our American friend, trying to be nice, leaned over and made conversation.

"You likee soup?" he asked the Oriental.

The Chinese fellow nodded his head.

"You likee stew?"

He nodded again.

As it turned out, the guest speaker at the dinner was our Oriental friend, who got up and delivered himself of a beautiful forty-minute address on the UN definition of encouragement to self-reliance by underdeveloped countries of the world. The speech was in flawless Oxford English.

He returned to his place at the head of the table, sat down, turned to our crying victim and asked:

"You likee speechee?"

"He's such a great speaker, I'd rather hear him speak than eat."

"Me, too. I sat at the head table with him. I've heard him eat."

"You heard my speech, Professor. Do you think it would improve my delivery if I followed the example of Demosthenes and practiced my diction and elocution with pebbles and marbles in my mouth?"

"I would recommend quick-dry cement."

"How did you like my last speech, Mr. Hardwood?"

"Was that your last? How smart of you."

Speaker to heckler:

"Sir, there are only three things that hiss—a goose, a snake, and a fool. Come forth and be identified."

"I hope I am not unduly trespassing on the time of this gathering?"

"No, but there is a vast difference between trespassing on time and encroaching on eternity."

Bud Kelland:

"As toastmaster, I have always believed it isn't my mission to be very entertaining. Indeed, I should strive to make my comments a little tedious, so that the remarks of the speaker will, by contrast, appear the more amusing. As I look around at the gathering of speakers scheduled to address you tonight, I perceive that I shall have to rise to new heights of boredom."

"I noticed that chap making jottings during my speech. I was only one-quarter into my address when he stopped writing. I wonder why?"
"Maybe he was just writing down the ideas."

"This Union Hall is so noisy and there are so many interruptions that I can hardly hear myself talk."
"Don't worry Brother Harrison. . . . You ain't missin' nuthin'."

". . . And so, ladies and gentlemen, all that I am, or ever will be, I owe to my dear sweet mother."
From the back row: "Why don't you send her two bits and settle the account?"

The guest speaker didn't show. The entertainment committee went into a quick huddle and decided to call on one of their own members to "fill in." Their unanimous choice was Professor Wilf Illin, who declined.

"I'm not a public speaker," apologized the professor. "I've never spoken before an audience in my life. Sorry, I can't do it."

The toastmaster was instructed to introduce the professor anyway. It was assumed that once placed in a position like that, he would have to accommodate the audience.

"And now, ladies and gentlemen," said the toastmaster, "here is our own Professor Wilf Illin with his address."

"Thank you for that nice invitation, Bill," said the professor. "My address is 567A Northumberland Crescent, Cleveland, Ohio. Thank you."

Will Rogers, after long-winded speaker:
"You have just listened to the famous Chinese statesman, On Too Long."

And here, probably the worst case on record of a wipeout of a guest speaker.

The man had carefully prepared his speech to be delivered at the local theater on the occasion of his triumphant return to his place of birth after an absence of about thirty-five years. What he didn't realize, and what the entertainment committee didn't realize, was that two whole new generations had grown up in the town since the departure of the local boy who made good. People and times change.

As he launched into his address he had the crowd. After twenty minutes or so, some of the audience were noticeably fidgety. After half an hour the audience was paying little attention, and a few were leaving. By the time he had reached the one-hour point in his talk, two-thirds of the audience had left the theater and others were making signs of preparation for departure.

An usher slipped him a note as he frantically tried to find a way to cut his prepared speech short. The note read:

"Dear Mr. Harvison, When you have finished your speech, please be sure to turn off all the lights in the theater, lock the door to your dressing room, and slip the key under the door of the manager's office.

"Goodnight."

". . . If I've said anything to insult you . . . be assured, I meant to. . . ."

Rule: If you are in the audience of a theater or club watching a professional comic do his stuff and you get the urge to trade insults with him . . . forget it. You'll lose. He can make you look foolish every time. For every line you throw at him, he's ready with ten of his own, carefully filed away in his memory box for people just like you.

The *Montreal Star*'s Bruce Taylor tells about a night "at the old Chez Paree in Montreal when Billy Vines lost his audience to an elegant blonde in a full-length mink coat who waltzed up to a ringside table and stood, obviously showing it off, in the glare of the spotlight that should have been on him. Vines allowed her to pose long enough to be sure everyone was looking at her, then cracked, 'Okay, ma'am, we've all seen it now, so why don't you sit down before someone asks how you earned it?'

"Vines used to have what he called his 'white-heat line' when all else failed against a frustrated comedian in the audience, who thought he could tell funnier stories, tried to drown him out. Vines would stop his show, sit on the stage in front of the man, and direct that the house lights be turned up. Then, in a folksy tone of voice, he'd tell the audience that, when he was a little boy, he lived on a farm. And on that farm was the meanest, orneriest, thick-headed mule that anyone had ever seen. It was his job, Vines would say, to hitch up the mule for plowing.

" 'One day, I just couldn't stand that mule any longer. I took a big two-by-four and sent him off to mule heaven. My mother was horrified. She said to me: "Billy, you oughtn't to have done that. You mark my words, one day that jackass will come back to haunt you." '

" 'Friends,' he'd say, staring right at the man who'd been giving him a hard time, 'I want you to know my mother was as right as she could be.' "

Taylor goes on:

"The comedians I envy aren't today's suave young breed of button-down collar humorists. The ones I'm talking about are their predecessors, the guys who worked their way up through the honky-tonk beer joints.

"Their audiences were strictly rough and tumble, and they learned the art of heckler-squelching, or they didn't survive. Young comics now are seldom exposed to that kind of training ground because most second-rate clubs have taken to dispensing with comedians; it's cheaper to hire strippers, topless waitresses, and go-go dancers. Most of the putdown lines they use were originated by, and stolen from, the old-timers. And, thankfully I suppose, the places they work now have generally better-behaved audiences, so they haven't learned to be as instinctively vicious to maintain control.

"For example, the veteran Joe E. Ross [of *Car 54 Where Are You?* fame] once reduced a woman to tears for repeatedly drawing attention away from him by asking her escort in a very loud voice: 'Isn't my face beautiful? Go on, look at it. Isn't it beautiful?'

" 'I'm looking at it,' Ross snarled in that gravelly voice

of his. 'And you know what I think, lady? You should let it come to a point and have it lanced.' "

Taylor was reminded of:

"The aging burlesque comic at Montreal's Gayety Theater, one night about fifteen years ago, who was interrupted time and again by a particularly rude character in the balcony. Finally, when he could stand him no longer, the comedian walked to the front of the stage and asked for the spotlight to be turned on the man. All eyes went to him. The house became quiet.

" 'There, ladies and gentlemen,' the old performer said softly, 'is one of the best arguments for birth control you'll ever see.' "

Here follows some of the best of the thousands of audience heckler stoppers, or wipeouts, used so devastatingly on those who would challenge a professional comic:

"Look, buddy, I couldn't warm up to you even if we were cremated together."

"That's okay, folks . . . let him have his fun tonight. Tomorrow he'll be back on the garbage truck."

"You know, mister, you have very funny material . . . in your suit!"

"Hey! That's very good . . . you know, you're funny . . . looking!"

To a bald heckler: "Excuse me, mister, would you mind turning your head down to dim?"

"Mister, why don't you lay off . . . you're gonna lose . . . you have the personality of a boil."

"Mister, you've got more nerve than an abscessed tooth."

". . . Ah, why don't you walk east 'til your hat floats."

". . . Ah, why don't you put your teeth in backwards and bite yourself in the throat."

"Mister, how would you like a blood test with some old razor blades?"

". . . He's the kinda guy who'll hide your teeth and then offer you corn on the cob."

". . . He's the kinda guy who'll put a rattlesnake in your pocket and then ask you for a match."

"You know, mister, you're dull, unfunny, and boring, but in spite of all that, you make me sick."

"Is that your nose or did your pants fall down?"

"Why don't you go out to the parking lot and smell my exhaust pipe?"

"I really shouldn't put him down like that . . . this boy is lousy with money. 'Course . . . he's lousy without it, too!"

"I'd like to run into you again . . . sometime, when you're walking and I'm driving."

"You have lots of funny lines . . . in your face."

"Why don't you gargle with cement and let it get hard."

"You're the kind of guy I'd like to leave in the middle of the Sahara with a big canteen of cool, clear, salt water."

"Why don't all you noisy people at that table form a club . . . and beat each other over the head with it?"

"You're the kind of broad I'd like to take home to smother."

". . . Say, that's a very nice jacket you're wearing there, fella. . . . Put the spotlight on that man so the folks can see. . . . There, isn't that some jacket, folks? Somewhere in this town there is a Peugeot with no seatcovers."

21

"I know your type . . . you're the kind of guy who sneaks into a fella's bedroom at two in the morning, removes the string from his pajamas, and yells: FIRE."

"Look, buddy, I've got only fourteen minutes to come out here and make a fool of myself . . . you've got all evening."

"What's wrong with you? Did you get up on the wrong side of the floor this morning?"

"There she is, folks . . . a sweetheart. Stand up and take a bow, honey. There is a girl who won't go anywhere without her mother . . . and her mother will go anywhere."

"Look, buddy, don't bug me while I'm working. . . . Would I come down to your place and take your shovel away?"

"Officer, would you remove that man in the cheap suit?"

"Okay, I'll give you time to do your bit. Do you want to stand up and be seen or lie down and be recognized?"

"Why don't you wait 'til after the show, buddy? You can come back to my dressing room and we'll have a nice man-to-jerk talk."

"Hey . . . that's a very unusual hat you're wearing, lady. . . .What happened, couldn't the man guess your weight?"

"Mister, you have all the charm of a temporary filling."

"It's so comforting having someone like you in the audience . . . something like . . . having a parachute on a submarine."

"You're about as entertaining as one wrestler."

"Oh, oh! . . . must be a full moon tonight, folks."

"I can see you're the straight-and-narrow type . . . a straight figure and a narrow mind."

"There y'are folks . . . there is an example of what happens when first cousins intermarry."

"Hey! Didn't I just see your picture on a bottle of iodine?"

"Mister, why don't you quit while it's still up to you?"

"Madam, do I go to YOUR place of business and turn off your red light?"

"Don't feel bad. A lot of people have no talent."

"Why don't you quit, buddy? You're about as popular here tonight as a cactus in a nudist colony."

". . . Given an audience, there is no act too noble or too daring.
Without the gallery, things are different. . . ."

    —WINSTON CHURCHILL

Sir Winston Churchill, the indefatigable politician, statesman, historian, artist, sailor, orator, and wipeout specialist.

His squelches were invariably powerful and effective, but rarely vicious or destructive. Oftentimes he could thwart an adversary without uttering a word. His favorite trick in the House of Commons for years involved his famed giant "Churchill Cigars."

When an unpleasant MP, one that Churchill wished to distract during his address, took the floor, Churchill would light up and create a smoke screen that could have saved the Maginot Line. Churchill would lovingly puff away at his stogie, allowing the ash to become longer and longer until it was several inches in length! Both sides of the House would find themselves more involved in watching the progress of Sir Winston's cigar than in the speech from the floor.

It was years later that Sir Winston revealed how he managed the trick. He claimed he could keep a four-inch ash on his cigar from falling to the floor by first piercing the cigar full length with a long hat pin!

He was once asked how he had enjoyed a weekend as a guest at the castle of an unnamed duke and duchess.

"Well, I shall tell you," replied Winston. "If the wine had been as old as the chicken, and the maid as willing as the duchess, I should have had a marvelous weekend."

He would not hesitate to be brutally honest at some-one's expense . . . particularly someone he considered hostile to his person. . . .

He was once invited to a gathering by an unpleasant woman he knew to be a social climber and a user.

He sent his would-be hostess the following wire: RE-GRET I CANNOT COME TONIGHT. CONTRIVED EXCUSE FOLLOWS.

During World War II, Churchill attended the funeral of a very senior civil servant who had been killed in one of the German air raids.

An overly ambitious office-seeker took Winston aside and asked if he could please replace the deceased official.

"I have no objection, my good man," boomed Churchill, "if the funeral director will agree to the switch."

Churchill's great wit and command of language were with him from the day he entered the British House of Commons as a young member.

Once, in the early years, Churchill was delivering a hard, direct speech in the House, when suddenly an out-raged member of the opposition jumped to his feet to protest. Alas, all that would fall out of his mouth were a few machine-gun bursts of rage in the form of incoherent sputters.

Churchill stopped, waited for the man to sit down, and then addressed the House again with: "My honorable friend should not develop more indignation than he can contain."

I suppose most of us could, if called upon and given sufficient time, compose an adequate, if not scholarly, rebuttal to an accusation of some sort. The beautiful Winston did it brilliantly . . . without hesitation.

Early in his career, a Colonel Kenyon-Slaney once accused him on the floor of the House of being a traitor.

Churchill took the floor, unsheathed his greatest weapon, his instant rhetoric, and hacked away:

"I've noticed that when political controversy becomes excited, persons of choleric dispositons and limited intelligence are apt to become rude.

"If I was a traitor, at any rate, I was fighting the Boers in South Africa when Colonel Kenyon-Slaney was slandering them at home. I had the honor of serving in the field for our country while this gallant, fire-eating colonel was content to kill Kruger with his mouth in the comfortable security of England."

There was no way a man could have the last word with Churchill. Members of the House would rise, take the floor of the House, and direct a carefully planned and worded question at the Prime Minister. Invariably, they regretted it.

After the war, shortly after re-election to power in 1951, to show the people good faith, Sir Winston reduced his own salary and the salaries of many ministers and officials.

Mr. W. Watt, Labor MP, sarcastically directed a question to Churchill:

" 'Is it not a fact that when income tax has been deducted the saving is relatively negligible, and would it not be more appropriate if at his time of life the Prime Minister abandoned these cheap demagogic gestures?'

"Churchill answered immediately, 'I think the Honorable Gentleman is a judge of cheap demagogic gestures, but they do not often come off when he makes them.'

"Mr. Shinwell, Labor MP, took the floor.

" 'In view of the castigations of the Right Honorable Gentleman on the members of the former government, does he not realize that, even at the reduced salary, the members of his government are not worth it?'

"Churchill shot back: 'The Right Honorable Gentleman is no doubt trying to live up to the cheap demagogic gestures mentioned by his Honorable Friend.' "

(from *Hansard*, July 29, 1952)

A member of his government once crossed the floor to sit on the left with the Labor Party.

Winston's comment?

"This, gentlemen, is the first time I have ever seen a rat swimming TOWARD a sinking ship."

Churchill had devised, besides his cigar routine mentioned earlier, effective ways to distract a speaker or the audience or both.

During a speech by Sir William Joynson-Hicks, Churchill shook his head vigorously until a very distracted and confused Joynson-Hicks stopped in the middle of his speech, glared at Churchill, and announced:

"I see my Right Honorable friend shaking his head. I wish to remind him that I am only expressing my own opinion."

"And I," replied Churchill, "wish to remind the speaker that I am only shaking my own head."

Another Churchillian diversionary tactic in the House was a simple one. He destroyed a speech of Hugh Gaitskell's with it in 1952.

Mr. Gaitskell had the floor and was delivering an address on economic affairs. It became apparent that the members were following Gaitskell's speech with intense interest. He was scoring points and obviously hurtling toward a succinct and clean conclusion.

Suddenly, Churchill made his move. He began frantically searching through the pockets of his pants and vest. He searched the floor in front of him, checked behind his bench, and went through his pants pockets again.

Just a few members noticed what was happening at first. Soon, Churchill's frantic search had the entire House, including the public gallery, intensely interested in his behavior.

Gaitskell became uneasy. He hesitated, then stopped. He had lost the House.

Churchill had done it again.

Later, feigning ignorance of the devastating effect his scheme had caused, he shrugged:

"I was only looking for my jujube."

Churchill once referred to the socialist regime in Britain as a "government of the duds by the duds and for the duds." He went on to predict the socialists would disappear "unwept, unhonored, unsung, and unhung."

Often the target of Churchill's scalding tongue was Welshman Aneurin Bevan (Labor MP for Ebbw Vale).

Answering questions on the government's recognition of Red China, the Prime Minister said:

"As we had great interests there, and also on general grounds, I thought that it would be a good thing to have diplomatic representation. But, if you recognize anyone, it does not necessarily mean that you like him. We all, for instance, recognize the Right Honorable member for Ebbw Vale."

He is reported to have once referred to Sir Stafford Cripps as Sir Stifford Crapps. Sir Stafford Cripps was one of Churchill's pet aversions and favorite targets for destruction.

In 1946, in the House, he said:

"None of his [Cripps] colleagues can compare with him in that acuteness and energy of mind with which he devotes himself to so many topics injurious to the strength and welfare of the state."

Has Churchill ever been at a total loss for words? Only once. It happened early in his career, at a point when the Conservative party became disenchanted with the young rebel in their midst.

A young Conservative, Claude Lowther, once excitedly informed the House that the dread disease, beriberi, had broken out in South Africa. He went on to say he was sure Churchill had contracted the disease because one of the symptoms was a terrific swelling of the head.

Churchill gave no answer. He got up, crossed the floor of the House, and sat on the Liberal side.

No one escaped Churchill's paring knife, not even his beloved "Clemmie."

Churchill's monster cigars were with him everywhere . . . even in bed. When Lady Churchill finally complained about the burns on the sheets, Sir Winston sent for a pair of scissors and snipped out all the charred spots.

Did Sir Winston inherit his instant wipeout power from his American mother, Jenny Jerome?

She invited George Bernard Shaw to dinner. Shaw refused to go, saying:

"What have I done to provoke such an attack on my well-known habit?" (Shaw hated parties.)

Churchill's mother answered:

"I know nothing about your habits. I hope they are not as bad as your manners!"

Shaw once sent Winston Churchill two tickets to an opening night performance of one of his plays with a note that read:

"Here is a ticket for you and one for a friend—if you have one."

Churchill sent back this message:

"I regret I cannot make it on the first night, but will try to make it on the second—if there is one."

He was informed one day, just before entering the House, that a front bencher, one particularly hostile to Churchill, was ill in the hospital.

"Dear me," said Churchill. "I do hope it's nothing trivial."

It was at the time of Sir Winston's leadership during World War II that many systems changed in the military. In many instances, for example, even enlisted men were let in on tactics, briefings, and objectives.

An aging general of the British army expressed his distaste for this new system. "Why, Mr. Prime Minister, after all, it is a fact that familiarity breeds contempt."

"My dear sir," said Churchill, "I beg you to consider that without a certain amount of familiarity, it is practically impossible to breed anything."

". . . A political war is one in which everyone shoots from the lip. . . ."
   —RAYMOND MOLEY

A delicious squelch came to our ears from the southern states. A young man, carrying a placard calling for equality for the American Negro and a halt to American brush-fire wars, was attacked by a woman with an umbrella. A large crowd gathered and she demanded between blows on the young man's head:

"What kind of an American are you? Shame. . . . Where are you from? Where were you born, and WHERE DID YOU GROW UP?"

"I was born right here in Mississippi, m'am," the boy answered politely. He then raised his trouser cuff, exposed a false leg, and added, "But I grew up in Viet Nam!"

Friend to reporter: "You're planning to ask the President what we're doing in Viet Nam? He doesn't even know what we're doing in the United States."

A politician inundated his ward with circular letters soliciting campaign funds. Each letter was simply addressed to "Occupant."

After about the seventh general mailing, a check in the

amount of $5,000 arrived in the mail. Overjoyed, he looked quickly at the signature to see who had been so generous. The check was signed "Occupant."

"Do you like conceited politicians as much as the other kind?"

"What other kind?"

A wipeout greeting card available now in the U.S.A.:
On the front cover: "Just because you're a Democrat doesn't mean you're odd or obnoxious."
Inside, it adds: "Stupid, maybe, but not odd or obnoxious."

"One thing I like about politics Russian-style. In your country, Ivan, when a politician is through, he's through."

"And in America," Ivan says, "there is one thing I like about your politicians. When they're bought, they stay bought."

Scrawled under hawk candidate's picture in San Francisco:
VOTING FOR THIS MAN MAY BE HAZARDOUS TO YOUR HEALTH.

". . . And so my friends, you may ask where I stand on the issues of today. . . ."
Heckler: "Aside!"

A congressman, invited to debate at a university forum, got this from a sophomore:
"I think politicians can be closely compared with contraceptives. They give you a sense of security while you're being screwed."

French official at diplomatic cocktail party in Washington:

"Yes, in France there must be some control exercised over the riffraff who sneer at the law. I am glad to see, at last, that my government is taking a firm stand on these matters. Why just this past weekend, a young student was arrested for running down the Champs Elysees shouting, 'De Gaulle is wrecking France. De Gaulle is wrecking France!' "

"They arrested him just for that?"

"But, yes."

"What was the charge? Revealing state secrets?"

"Well, election time will soon be here. I plan to run for office again, my friends . . . and I guess the air will soon be full of my speeches."

"Yeah . . . and vice versa."

Also, during the 1968 Presidential nomination campaign, Eugene McCarthy was accused by a fellow Democrat:

"You know what you're trying to do? We're wise to you. You're trying to split the Democratic party!"

To which McCarthy replied: "My friend, have you ever tried to split sawdust?"

Ad published in Greenwich Village weekly a week before the election:

FURNISHED ROOM FOR RENT. NO BATHROOM FACILITIES. SUITABLE FOR DEMOCRAT.

Nobody got squelched more in this past half-century than Barry Goldwater during his shot at the Presidency. The main theme of Goldwater putdowns were invariably about his "living in the past!"

One reporter claimed he saw Goldwater out swimming one day and his bathing suit had a hole . . . in the knee!

There was a story circulating that Goldwater would be featured on an evening TV show. It would be scheduled on Tuesday nights from 7 to 6:30.

One female reporter in Washington wrote: "Senator Barry Goldwater is so conservative that he even frowns on topless bathing suits . . . for men!"

Emmet Watson in the *Seattle Post-Intelligencer:* "It's easy to recognize the Goldwater bandwagon . . . it's the one with the stone wheels."

And the gag reported by Dick Hitt in the *Dallas Times-Herald:*

A patient had just come-to at a New York hospital after thirteen months in a coma. It was during the great blackout. He took one look at the darkened city and muttered: "Uh, oh . . . I guess Goldwater won the election, huh?"

And, finally, this wire Goldwater received from a voter:
HAVING A WONDERFUL TIME IN 1840. WISH YOU WERE HERE.

". . . And so I say, ladies and gentlemen, we all have cause for concern. Automation is taking away your jobs . . . yes, and MY job too. I can see the day when computers will one day even replace us politicians!"

Heckler: "Impossible! Where ya gonna find a machine that breaks promises?"

Senator being shown through a factory producing novelty items. He stops at the workbench of a young man building what looks like a horse.

"But," said the senator to the young man, "you seem to

37

be building just the front end of these horses. Why is that?"

"You're right, sir. . . . We build just the front ends . . . then we ship them off to Washington for final assembly."

"I wouldn't vote for you if you were St. Peter himself."

"If I were St. Peter, sir, you wouldn't be in my ward."

Art Buchwald on the infamous telegram incident:

"Gov. Reagan started reading the telegram and suddenly realized it wasn't for him. So he did the only honorable thing and had it xeroxed and distributed to the press."

". . . And so I repeat, ladies and gentlemen, knowledge is power."

"That's right, senator . . . and you sure know the right things about the right people."

". . . And in conclusion, ladies and gentlemen, let me say this. In spite of what my political opponent sitting on the stage here secretly thinks about you all, I came here convinced that your parents are all married."

A fuming politician, who felt he had been badly treated by the local newspaper, hired teen-agers to do his dirty work.

All the city trash cans were labeled with: THIS BASKET FOR GARBAGE.

To this sign he had his hirelings add: AND THE BROCKVILLE TIMES.

The premier of a Canadian province had commented to some people in his circle at a victory party that this day marked the twelfth time the people of his province had returned him to power.

"I've been elected twelve times!" he said happily.

Someone, obviously from the enemy camp, quipped: "I guess, Mr. Premier, the people of this province are just going to keep electing you over and over again 'til you learn your job."

When Governor Romney of Michigan made his famous: "I was brainwashed by Washington" statement, someone close to the top said privately:

"The truth is, we *did* try to brainwash Romney, but we had nothing to work with."

Hubert Humphrey's inadvertent wipeout of Lyndon Johnson during the 1968 Presidential race:

"No sane person in this country likes the war in Viet Nam, and neither does President Johnson."

A Russian and an American in the UN cafeteria got into a heated discussion about the two different systems of government. The cafeteria fell quiet as the voices of the two men grew louder and louder. Realizing he now had the attention of about forty-five people, the American grabbed the opportunity for a putdown this way:

"I apologize, Mr. Polinoff, for the things I have said. Please let us part as good friends. Before I go, let me tell you a story: A Russian wolfhound met a cocker spaniel one day and they talked as they became acquainted.

" 'How do you like America?' the cocker spaniel asked the wolfhound.

" 'Well, it's different from where I come from. In the Soviet Union I eat bones dipped in vodka and caviar. I have my own split-level doghouse made of polished walnut with wall-to-wall broadloom. I sleep on a thick warm carpet of mink each night.'

" 'Well,' asked the cocker spaniel, 'if things were like that in Russia, why did you come to America?'

" 'Because,' replied the Russian wolfhound, 'I like to bark once in awhile.' "

And so saying, our friend left the cafeteria to a small round of applause from the diners.

Some wipeouts, when the victim is defenseless, are vicious . . . brutal.

In New York, under a poster of Robert McNamara, someone had scrawled: STOP ME, BEFORE I KILL AGAIN.

This story, supposedly true, came in across the Iron Curtain. It all takes place in a train compartment in Czechoslovakia. The stars in this play are a Czechoslovakian, a Russian officer, a little old lady, and a young attractive girl.

Shortly after the train enters a dark tunnel, the passengers hear first a kiss, then a loud and substantial slap.

The girl thinks: "Isn't that odd that the Russian tried to kiss the old lady and not me?"

The old lady thinks: "That is a good girl with fine morals."

The Russian officer thinks: "That Czech is a smart fellow. He steals a kiss and I get slapped."

The Czech thinks: "I am really smart. I kiss the back of my hand, clout a Russian officer, and get away with it!"

A four-star wipeout took place in Toronto, Canada, some years ago when a well-known labor leader of that great city introduced the very vocal Mayor Philip Givens this way:

"We're very proud, brothers, to have as our guest afterdinner speaker His Worship, The Mayor, Phil Givens. I've known Phil for years and have heard him speak at numerous banquets and dinners. Funny thing about him . . . you put in a dinner and up comes a speech."

The mayor took the podium. "I'd like to thank my old 'friend' for his introduction and comments. It is quite true that, as Mr. Harris told you, I'm peculiar that way. Put in a dinner and up comes a speech. However, gentlemen, I am sure you will agree, that is preferable to Mr. Harris' problem which is the opposite.

"In his case, he puts in a speech and up comes your dinner!"

Politician at rally:

"There are dozens and dozens of houses of prostitution in this town. ....

"As mayor of this city, I am proud to say I have never been in one of them."

"Which one, Mayor Bill?" called out a voice from the back row.

A midwestern weekly hit the streets with a scathing editorial on the local administration under the large banner:

HALF OF OUR LEGISLATORS ARE CROOKS.

Many local politicians were outraged and demanded a retraction, to which the editor agreed. Next week a four-banner headline appeared on the front page that read:

HALF OF OUR LEGISLATORS ARE NOT CROOKS.

During the question-answer period, a gentleman in the back row requested the floor and asked the political candidate the following:

"Mr. Speaker, you referred to yourself several times during your speech as a successful politician. My dear old silvery-haired dad always told us kids that a successful politician is a fellow who finds out how the people are going, then takes a shortcut across a field, gets out in front, and makes them think he is leading the way. Is that an accurate definition would you say?"

A furious alderman in a small midwestern town storms into the office of the local paper, bullies his way past the editor's secretary, barges into the editor's office, and demands:

"Was it your rag of a paper that reported I was a crooked politician and a scoundrel?"

"I'm sure it wasn't, Mr. Bebee. It must have been *The Globe.* We never print stale news."

Spencer Tracy, before his death, to a political organizer, who was defending the trend of actors entering public office:

"Before you ask any more actors to get into politics, just remember who shot Lincoln!"

At a small intimate Washington gathering in the home of a senator, a loud crashing noise from upstairs startled the group into silence.

"By George," whispered the senator. "I think there's a thief in the house."

"Not possible," whispered back a member of the House of Representatives. "In the Senate perhaps, but the House, NEVER!"

Georgie Jessel, commissioned to speak on behalf of President Roosevelt in a nationwide broadcast, had been allotted twelve minutes to speak. Preceding speakers had exceeded their time limit and Jessel found himself with ninety seconds remaining at the end of the broadcast.

He scared the devil out of the gathered Democrats with this hastily prepared speechette:

"Ladies and gentlemen, most of my eloquent colleagues have this evening taken up much of their time in expounding the weaknesses and vices of President Roosevelt's opponent, Thomas Dewey. I shall not. I could not do this. I

42

know Governor Thomas E. Dewey, and Mr. Dewey is a fine man."

A low murmur of disapproval spread through the assembled crowd.

Jessel went on: "Yes, Dewey is a fine man. So is my Uncle Morris. My Uncle Morris shouldn't be President; neither should Dewey. Goodnight."

A head of cabbage once landed at the feet of William Howard Taft as he campaigned for the Presidency.

"Ah," noted Taft to his delighted audience. "I see one of my adversaries has lost his head."

Herb Caen in the *San Francisco Chronicle* tells this delicious tale about the mayor:

When a department head isn't moving fast enough, the mayor phones him and says:

"Congratulations, you have just been elected to the Goya Club."

"Why THANK you, Mr. Mayor," the official replies. "But what is the Goya club?"

"It's G.O.Y.A., Goya," explains the mayor icily. "GET OFF YOUR ASS!"

The mayor had exerted great pressure on the alderman to change his vote on a municipal re-zoning bylaw.

In council, after the vote, the mayor rose and said:

"Well, George, I'm glad you voted our way. You've finally seen the light."

"I didn't see the light, Mr. Mayor," the alderman snapped. "I felt the heat."

Heywood Broun was once assigned to interview a political figure who had the personality and intelligence of a crowbar.

"I have nothing to say," offered the official.

"I know that," snapped Broun. "Now shall we begin with the interview?"

Two would-be wheels in Washington were discussing their "pull" with the President. Their guest from Toledo listened quietly.

Number One: "Why just last week I was invited to the White House for tea and a private chat with the President of the United States."

Number Two: "That's nothing. I was there a couple of days ago with the President, right in his office, when suddenly the HOT LINE rang . . . and you know he didn't interrupt our conversation to answer it!"

Guest: "I know you won't believe this, chaps, but I was with the President in his office this very morning. The HOT LINE rang and the President *did* answer it. It was for me."

The President, on a trans-oceanic call to Paris:

"May I speak with the President of France, please? This is the President of the United States speaking."

"I am sorry, Mr. President, General de Gaulle departed early this morning on a tour of countries friendly to France. Please call again when he returns."

"Very well," said the President. "I'll call back at noon!"

There is a famous story about Senator Hayden of the State of Arizona. William White, then correspondent for *The New York Times,* got word that the senator wished to have a word with him. This made White a happy man. The senator practically never talked to the press, and an interview with Hayden would be a coup for White.

He jumped into a taxi and, pad and pencil in hand, breathlessly burst into the senator's office.

"I hear you want to see me, Senator. I'm William White, *New York Times.*"

"Why, yes, I do, young man. Ever since I came to Washington, I've been reading *The Times* . . . I like it very much. I've finally decided that I'd like to be a regular reader. Can you take my subscription?"

"Can you contribute ten dollars to bury one of my political colleagues?"

"Here's twenty dollars. Bury two of them."

Bob Hope, on Hubert Humphrey: "He has so much to be modest about."

Aneurin Bevan once left the Conservative side of the British House of Commons speechless. It was during World War II. Bevan was criticizing the conduct of the invasion of Italy by the Allied forces. He described it thus:

"The Allied Command, approaching the conquest of Italy, can be likened to the old man approaching his young bride, fascinated, sluggish, and apprehensive."

In the course of a tirade against Winston Churchill, Bevan noticed Miss Florence Horsburgh, Minister of Education, smiling indulgently. This angered the fiery Socialist and he snapped:

"I do not know what the Right Honorable Lady, the Minister of Education, is grinning about. I was told by one of my honorable friends this afternoon that that is a face that sank a thousand scholarships."

Adlai Stevenson, during his Presidential campaign, once borrowed an old joke to make a point.

He told his large New York audience: "In this election, we offer the Republicans this deal. If they promise not to tell lies about us, we'll promise not to tell the truth about them."

45

"Prisoner at the bar. This is the fourth time in two weeks you have appeared before me for drunkenness and vagrancy. You're a disgrace to humanity. Have you ever earned a dollar in your entire life?"

"Yeah, I did, Judge. I voted for you in the last election."

Some people are moved to put EVERYONE down. Comedian Paul Gray put it this way before the election:

"Dean Rusk is a hawk, Eugene McCarthy is a dove, and President Johnson is a lame duck—politicians are for the birds."

When Spiro T. Agnew was named Richard Nixon's running mate, the Second City Revue in Chicago included a new number in their program.

An offstage voice announced: "We now present the highlights from the life of Spiro T. Agnew."

Then, for the next two minutes, the stage remained empty and nothing happened.

"... With the fearful strain that is on me night and day, if I did not laugh I should die...."
—ABRAHAM LINCOLN

One of history's greatest wipeout artists was Abe Lincoln. Not because he relished verbally squashing his fellow man. To him, it was a punishment, an eye for an eye.

No office in the world has heaped upon it more abuse and criticism than the office of the President of the United States. Newspapers, the public, political opponents . . . *everyone* has an opinion on the President . . . and they hesitate not to express it.

Because of his appearance, long, lean, with unusually large hands and feet, and because he occupied the President's office during one of America's most difficult times, Lincoln *had* to have a sense of humor. There are many stories of his good humor and patience, but there were times when even this man with the great heart resorted to a sharp tongue to deal with arrogance or inadequacy.

Early in his political career he was seeking votes among his neighbors. He found one old codger up in the hills near town who spoke his mind unhesitatingly:

"I wouldn't even think about it, Abe. I'd sooner vote for the devil."

"I am sure you would," said Lincoln quietly. "But in case your friend doesn't run, maybe you would give your vote to me."

During the Civil War, one of his generals, McClellan, delayed too long in sending his armies into Richmond. The delay became unbearable and Lincoln's advisers were pressing to take action immediately against the general. Lincoln's strategy was simple. He didn't remove the general from duty. This undoubtedly would create low morale among the troops. He moved McClellan to action by sending the following message:

"My Dear McClellan: If you don't want to use the army, I should like to borrow it for awhile."

As a young lawyer, Lincoln once questioned each juror in a case he was defending whether they were acquainted with the attorney appearing for the other side. When it became evident that at least three of the jurors did indeed know the attorney, the judge interrupted with:

"Mr. Lincoln, you are wasting the time of the court. The mere fact that a juror knows your opponent does not disqualify him."

"No, that's true, your honor," agreed Lincoln. "But I'm afraid that some of these gentlemen may *not* know him, which would place me at a disadvantage."

In an important trial being fought by Lincoln for a client, it was becoming increasingly evident that the outcome of the case would be decided mainly on the evidence offered by an eminent surgeon.

Lincoln didn't cross-examine the physician except to ask:

"Doctor, how much money will you receive for testifying in this case?"

The judge indicated that the question must be answered.

The doctor revealed an immense fee. The jury gasped.

Lincoln addressed the jury: "Gentlemen, big fee, big swear."

He won.

About a political opponent: "He can compress more words into the smallest ideas of any man I ever met."

When young Abe Lincoln was running for Congress, he waited on the platform while his political opponent, who had elected to speak first, went on and on in a very loud voice, booming out across the countryside a barrage of interminable shouting and gesticulating.

Then came Lincoln's turn. Approaching the lectern quietly, he looked out at his audience and began in a gentle, steady voice:

"Listening to the speech of my worthy opponent, I am reminded of a boat I once saw in my very young days. Back in the days when I performed my part as a keelboatman, I made the acquaintance of a trifling little steamboat which used to bustle and puff and wheeze about the Sangamon River. It had a five-foot boiler and a seven-foot whistle, and every time it whistled, it stopped."

Congressman Abraham Lincoln once attended a reception in his honor in Washington. Upon arriving, he placed his tall silk hat, open end up, on a chair in the corner of the small reception hall.

A lady, with a rather large physique and a particularly bountiful derriere, headed straight for the chair and sat down upon the hat, crushing it badly. Lincoln rushed over ... but too late. The damage had been done.

The woman, taking the hat, thrust it into Lincoln's hands and said indignantly: "Here . . . is this yours?"

"Yes it is, m'am, but I wish you hadn't done‾that. I could have told you my hat wouldn't fit you before you tried it on."

Some of his generals in the field got a little dramatic and perhaps even found the war glamorous. Lincoln had no time for this kind of man.

General Joe Hooker would, during combat, charge on horseback into the action leading his men, and send urgent messages back to the President on the "state of the war." Invariably he signed these dispatches with:

"General J. Hooker—Headquarters in the Saddle."

After about a dozen of these "Headquarters-in-the-Saddle" messages, Lincoln . . . and history doesn't record whether he sent this on to the general or not . . . said:

"The trouble with Hooker is that he has his headquarters where his hindquarters ought to be!"

Abe Lincoln was often quite candid about the performance of some of the generals who fought the American Civil War for the Union. He once got word that a brigadier general and twelve army mules had been captured by the Confederates.

"Pity," observed Lincoln. "Those mules cost us two hundred dollars apiece."

On yet another occasion, he again showed his dissatisfaction with most of his generals. One of them once whispered in Lincoln's ear that General Grant was consuming large quantities of whisky.

"Find out immediately what brand Grant is drinking. I'd like to send some to my other generals."

Seeking favors, people often anonymously dispatched gifts to President Lincoln. Only later would the sender reveal himself to a committed President. This was a source of great annoyance to him.

One day a letter arrived on Lincoln's desk inquiring how Mr. Lincoln had enjoyed the case of wine the sender had presented.

Lincoln wrote back:

"Sir, I thank you for your letter which finally enables me to thank you for your gift. Believe me, I have tried every kind of insect poison and found nothing to equal your Old Dry Cabinet."

". . . When you have no basis for an argument, abuse the plaintiff. . . ."
—CICERO

In Kingston, Canada, the Crown Prosecutor, T. J. Rigney, was, in his younger years, a pretty tough and overly rough prosecuting attorney. He made many enemies with his pressure on witnesses, never letting up from the moment they took the stand.

He usually managed to get in the last word. The same magistrate, a pal of Rigney's, occupied the Kingston Bench for a long, long time. Rigney could do no wrong.

A traffic accident case was being heard in the Kingston courthouse. One of the witnesses was Dick Herrington, who later became a city alderman.

Rigney was really pressing Herrington for the seemingly most insignificant details of the accident he had witnessed.

"If there were an imaginary line down the middle of the road . . . how far from the imaginary line did the plaintiff's car come to rest?"

Herrington thought for a moment and said, "Oh I imagine. . . ."

"Don't imagine!" barked Rigney. "How far from the imaginary line was the car?"

"Well, sir," offered Herrington, "if it is an imaginary

line, I can only imagine how far the car would be from it."

Rigney sat down.

In a similar case described by Montreal's Crown Prosecutor, Louis Freedman, a self-styled, brow-beating, would-be Nizer pressed the witness with:

". . . And tell the court *exactly* how far the car was from the fire hydrant on the northeast corner of Bishop and Stanley streets."

"The car," offered the witness with a twinkle in his eye, "was exactly 15 yards, 11 feet, 14¾ inches from the hydrant."

"How can the witness be so specific in his reply?" demanded the attorney.

"Because the witness assumed that some idiot lawyer would demand to know the exact distance . . . so I measured it."

In Winston Churchill's *Great Contemporaries,* he tells of a lovely wipeout executed by the First Earl of Birkenhead in a court of British law.

The earl and the sitting judge had bombarded each other with some barbed exchanges . . . each time, the earl surfaced as the absolute victor.

Enraged, the judge finally sputtered: "Young man, you are extremely offensive."

"As a matter of fact," replied the earl, "we both are, but I'm *trying* to be and you can't help it."

"Does the defendant really expect this court of law to accept his story that the completely assembled still on his property was not being used for the purpose of producing illicit whisky?"

"That's right, your honor. I bought that as a novelty, a conversation piece. I do not now, nor have I ever, operated it as a still to produce whisky."

55

"Hogwash! As far as this court is concerned, possession of the equipment is proof enough of your guilt."

"Well, it seems then, your honor, that you'd better also charge me with raping your daughter."

"Did you rape my daughter?"

"No, sir. But she was at my place last night and I certainly have the equipment for it."

"And what do you do, sir?"

"I'm a criminal lawyer, sir."

"Aren't they all?"

"Soon as I realized what a crooked business law is, I got out of it."

"Yes? How much?"

"You are a dirty liar and a shyster," screamed one lawyer at the other.

"And you," yelled the other, "are a two-bit cheat and a crook."

"Well, now that the counselors have identified themselves properly," intoned the judge, "let the case begin."

A witness kept answering questions with: "Well, I think. . . ."

"Don't think," interrupted the lawyer. "Tell us what you know, not what you think."

"Well, I'm not a lawyer," she shot back. "I can't talk without thinking."

I WANT to tell the truth, but every time I try, some lawyer objects.

". . . There is no satisfaction in hanging a man who does not object to it. . . ."

—GEORGE BERNARD SHAW

It is the century's understatement to inform you that George Bernard Shaw spoke his piece and feared no one.

George Bernard Shaw was constantly lapeled everywhere he went by people who "knew him when." A matronly and gushing female once drooled at him:

"Oh, Mr. Shaw . . . I don't know if you remember me, but many years ago, when I was a young girl, you asked me to marry you."

"Oh?" droned Shaw. "And . . . did you?"

One of Shaw's best-known and most oft told squelches came on a day when a lovely lady of the stage, Ellen Terry, declared:

"Just think if we were to have children, you and I, how wonderful a combination that would be for a child to have my beauty and your brains."

"Yes, my dear," replied Shaw acidly. "But what a tragedy if the poor infant had my beauty and *your* brains."

Shaw once squelched a heckler in his audience with:

"I wholeheartedly agree with your sentiments, my dear sir. But what are you and I against so many millions?"

A visitor once expressed surprise to Shaw that he didn't have a single vase of flowers anywhere in the house.

"I thought you loved beautiful things," said his guest. "Yet I don't see any flowers."

Shaw's famous short temper cracked. He glared at the man and snapped:

"Sir, I am also very fond of children, but I don't cut off their heads and stick them in pots around the house!"

I'm not sure who got put down here. I'm not even sure it's a genuine putdown, but it's a good line by Shaw, so, in it goes:

". . . Fish and relatives begin to smell after three days."

Shaw once chose to denigrate, in the strongest, brutal Shavian fashion, everything American. The tables were turned on him. His campaign against the U.S.A. caused most of the American press to rise to the defense of Uncle Sam, and they had their daily Shaw lynchings on their pages.

One editor of a major American paper held back and waited 'til Shaw came to the U.S.A. with Mrs. Shaw. The editor covered the story this way:

"Mrs. George Bernard Shaw arrived in this country early yesterday and immediately was launched on a mad tour of luncheons and dinner parties. Mrs. Shaw attended the theater in the evening and retired to the Waldorf at 1:00 A.M. We welcome Mrs. Shaw to our great land.

"Mrs. Shaw was accompanied by her husband, George Bernard Shaw, a writer."

He once received an engraved invitation that read:

"Lady Joel Hindmarsh will be at home Friday between seven and nine."

Underneath, Shaw scribbled: "George Bernard Shaw, likewise." And sent it back.

Shaw hated dinner parties, cocktail parties, or any gathering of more than four or five people.

The hostess at one party in his honor asked:

"Are you enjoying yourself, Mr. Shaw?"

"Yes I am," snapped Shaw. "And that is all I'm enjoying."

He hated many things, but most of all reporters, who in his late years pestered him frequently for interviews.

A young reporter managed to get the great man on the phone.

"How are you, Mr. Shaw?" he opened.

"Young man, when you are my age, you are either well or dead, good day!"

Shaw once attended a private concert in his capacity as critic. His hostess demanded to know what he thought of the violinist she had personally discovered.

Shaw smiled and observed: "He reminds me of Paderewski, madam."

After a moment of reflection, his hostess said: "But, Mr. Shaw, Paderewski is not a violinist. He's a pianist."

"Quite so, madam, quite so," said Shaw, grabbing his hat.

Cornelia Otis Skinner received a wire from Shaw the day after her opening in a revival of his *Candida*.

EXCELLENT, GREATEST, praised the wire.

She wired back: UNDESERVING SUCH PRAISE.

Shaw answered: I MEANT THE PLAY.

SO DID I, squashed Miss Skinner's final wire.

"...Speak oftly and carry a big lip...."
—GIANNI SCINGILLI

No one has been able to give a satisfactory explanation for it, but women who dislike each other, even a little, delight in slamming each other down, especially in public places. Here are some examples of cold-blooded wipeouts:

"Darling, I see you have a new hat."

"Yes, when I'm down in the dumps, I always get myself a new hat."

"I was wondering where you got those things from."

"There's that Mrs. Sprightly, who just moved in the neighborhood. My husband says she has a very magnetic personality."

"She ought to have. Everything she has on is charged."

"I've been a good horsewoman since I can remember. . . . My friends tell me when I ride, I'm like part of the animal."

"Oh? Which part?"

"Well, at least one thing you have to admit, I have an open mind."

"Yes, and a mouth to match."

"How do you like it, girls? It's just a little something I threw on."

"Looks like you missed."

"Wrinkled? Her face would hold a three-day rain."

"And when I was sixteen, girls, the President of the United States presented me with a beauty award."

"Really? I didn't think Lincoln bothered with that sort of thing."

One of the most often squelched young ladies of this decade has been British style-setter, Twiggy.

"Twiggy was charged in court yesterday for wearing a topless bathing suit, but she was acquitted."

"Insufficient evidence?"

"Her living bra committed suicide. It was leading an empty life."

"Twiggy looks like Sophia Loren after taxes."

"If it weren't for her Adam's apple, she'd have no shape at all."

"Twiggy sticks out her tongue, stands sideways, and looks like a zipper."

"If she didn't have warts, that strapless dress wouldn't stay up."

"If Twiggy was alive, she'd be a very sick lady."

"The only way she can get color in her face is to stick her tongue out."

"Twiggy needs suspenders to keep up her girdle."

"I'm surprised you would ask, Esmeralda. I'm thirty-three. Don't you think I'm lucky to look like this at thirty-three?"
"I think you're twice as lucky as you say you are."

"Oh, girls, look at the lovely pearls George bought me for my birthday. They're real, you know."
"Oh, I bet if I were to bite one of those pearls, I could prove they aren't real."
"Maybe you could, but for that you'd need real teeth."

"Darling, I was just wondering why you weren't invited to the Ducharme's party last week."
"Isn't that a coincidence, I was just wondering why you were."

"Oh, Sarah, I completely forgot about your little party last night."
"Weren't you there?"

"Hey, girls! Look at the new diamond bracelet George gave me. Isn't that beautiful?"
"That's lovely, Sarah. I can remember when that was part of the chandelier at the Bonaventure Hotel."

Beverley, showing ring: "Look, girls. What do you think?"
"Very nice. It's a Buck Rogers super-decoder, isn't it?"

"She's the world's leading amateur Human Being."

"Yeah? I'd like to see her kitchen sink. I bet that's stacked too."

There is nothing on this earth that will inspire women to do their worst than when one of their species arrives on the scene wearing a new fur coat. Here are a few overheard meows:

"I don't want to say how she got that coat, but I bet in six months she can't button it."

"Darling, you look like you were made for that coat. Why didn't you hold out for mink?"

"I would say she got that mink the same way minks get minks."

"I wonder if she got it to keep her warm or quiet."

"That's dyed mink? . . . To me it looks like it died a horrible death."

"Boy, I bet that set her back a few tantrums."

"The only thing that coat does for her is keep her warm."

"There goes a girl a guy can seduce even if he plays his cards *wrong.*"

"Sam says I look like a million."
"Right, dearie. All wrinkled and green."

"Sam says I have a contagious smile."
"Trench mouth?"

"Sam says I have a peach complexion."
"All yellow and fuzzy?"

"Oh, girls, look at the new brooch Bill Burroughs bought me."
"Careful, Marsha. Don't drop it. Seven years bad luck, you know."

"She has the knack of making strangers immediately."

"There goes Hermione. She claims she has a go-go mind."
"Yeah . . . and a so-so body."

"How do you like my new coat, girls?"
"Why it's lovely, June. Isn't it amazing what a good seamstress can do with a few old typewriter covers!"

"Joan, darling, guess what! I'm going to marry your old boyfriend, Tom Burke. He dresses so beautifully, don't you think?"
"Yes . . . and so quickly."

". . . And this, girls, is a portrait of one of my family's ancestors."
"Very nice, Katherine," snipped one of the cats. "He almost became my ancestor about a week ago, but I was outbid at the auction."

"It's nice meeting old friends. A lot of people think I'm dead."
"Not if they look closely."

"I'm getting divorced, girls!"
"Oh? . . . Who's the lucky man?"

"She believes she's still as good at attracting men as she never was."

Boston bluenose: "Actually, my dear, my family's ancestry is very old. We date back to Oliver Cromwell's time. And you?"
"I don't know," she replied. "All *our* records were lost in the great flood."

". . . And do you know, I refused to marry Jim McManus a year ago, and he has been drinking ever since?"

"Isn't that carrying a celebration a little too far?"

"Hi, Margie! Joan and Marsha and I were just talking about you. We were wondering why it is you never married. Did you ever have the chance to marry?"

"Suppose you ask your husbands."

". . . And François, the great expert on beautiful women, told me that I can match my legs with Dietrich anytime."

"How can you match your legs with Dietrich, Marge? They don't even match each other."

"She has a wonderful way of keeping a secret . . . going."

"Lady, I pulled you over 'cause you were doing fifty miles an hour in a thirty-mile zone."

"Officer, before this goes any further, are you supposed to advise me of my constitutional rights first or am I supposed to advise you that my nephew is on the police commission?"

"Oh, girls, I've such exciting news. Last week, I was appointed to direct the membership drive at our country club."

"Isn't that interesting, Hilda," squelched one of her listeners. "And how many members have you driven out so far?"

She had married Mr. Creep of all time. A cold fish, a dull-witted bore. She was telling her girl friends, who had at one time or another dated this stalemate:

"What a thrill it was in Niagara Falls," she gushed. "It was so exciting!"

"What happened?" asked one of the girls. "Did you go over the Falls in a barrel?"

"When she was a little girl, she just wanted to grow up and spread good cheer. Instead, she just grew up and spread."

"Darling, how do you like my new outfit? It was made in London."

"Really? Did you swim back in it?"

"Do you like this gown? I wore it to the Johnson Wedding."

"Oh? Lyndon's or Luci's?"

"Our dog is just like one of the family."

"Really—which one?"

". . . And this, girls, is a picture of me twenty-nine years ago."

"Isn't that interesting. And who is that baby on your lap?"

". . . And there I was . . . drinking in the scene, with the giant abyss yawning before me."

"Was the abyss yawning before you got there?"

"This lace is over sixty years old."

"Really . . . over sixty years old. Did you make it yourself?"

"There go the Johnsons."

"Yes, they're a sweet couple . . . except for her."

"I don't look thirty-eight, do I?"
"Not anymore, no."

"Everyone says I got my good looks from my father."
"Oh? Is he a plastic surgeon?"

"Darling, don't try to tell me about that. I have a pho-
tographic mind."
"Yes . . . too bad it never developed."

"Say, we've just redecorated our beautiful home."
"Oh, you've installed new padding?"

"You know, girls, a lot of men are going to be miserable
when I marry."
"Really? . . . How many men are you going to marry?"

"I don't think success has gone to her head."
"No, just to her mouth."

"Are you still henpecking that poor husband of yours?"
"I do not henpeck my husband!"
"Listen, he'd be afraid to tell you he was sterile even if
you were pregnant."

"Oh, look, girls, here comes Alice, the little whine
maker."

"She's some gal. Very fickle. Falls madly in bed with
every man she meets."

"Hey, Jenny! Barbara just stole your new boyfriend!"
"May the bird of paradise neutralize her pill."

"Hey, girls! I just got back from Doctor Levitt's office. He says he thinks I'm going to have triplets. Isn't that something? You know that only happens once in every one million, eight hundred thousand times!"

"One million, eight hundred thousand times! My dear, how do you find time to do your housework?"

Two felines at cocktail party:

"Darling, how nice to see you in that dress again. By the way, how do you like my hair-do?"

"It looks like your parole came through just as the warden pulled the switch."

A female clerk in a large department store was spritzing perfume on customers as they walked by her cosmetics' counter. This was a sales promotion gimmick to introduce the latest perfumes from Paris.

Two men were about to be sprayed when one suddenly blurted:

"Here! Don't spray me with any of that! My wife will think I've been in a whore house."

"It's all right, sweetie, you can spray me," said the other. "My wife doesn't know what a whore house smells like."

Right after a searing sermon on the new morality, the Reverend Wilkins asked all virgins in the church to please stand. There was a stirring in the congregation, but nobody stood. After about thirty uncomfortable seconds, a young woman with a baby in her arms struggled to her feet.

"You misunderstand, madam," explained Wilkins. "I asked only virgins to stand up."

"Well," said the woman, "you don't expect a two-month-old baby girl to stand up by herself, do you?"

70

Five bank bandits had just ordered the staff to lie on the floor, when one female teller shouted to another:

"Face down, dearie, this is a holdup not the office party."

Women often employ tricks on the subway or bus to shame men into giving them their seats. Sometimes it doesn't pay. I heard of one incident on the Toronto subway that ranks among the greatest of wipeouts.

This fellow had managed to get a seat after a really rough day delivering the mail. A beautifully tailored young woman he had never seen before, all decked out with jewelry and obviously out on a shopping trip, pulled this one. She leaned up to him and in a voice loud enough for everyone to hear said:

"Why, Gerry Barker! How nice to see you again. Boy, am I tired."

Well, our friend, whose name, of course, was not Gerry Barker, got the pitch and immediately surrendered his seat to the lady. Standing directly in front of her, he said in a very loud voice for all to hear:

"Why, Martha, do sit down . . . you must be so tired scrubbing floors day after day. By the way, don't bother coming to clean our house tomorrow. Make it Thursday instead. My wife is visiting the Premier tomorrow and she's going to try and get a stay of execution for your brother."

A lovely little blonde sitting at a bar being hounded by a lush at the next stool:

"C'mon honey, let's play," he said. "I wanna play, sweetie . . . care to join me?"

Finally after about an hour of this she said:

"Okay, let's play. Tell you what, we'll play horse. I'll play the front end, and you stay as sweet as you are."

This is supposed to have happened back in the 20's, when it was still considered bad form for women to smoke in public.

An elderly lady was sitting next to a young girl who was smoking at a lunch counter in a department store. Not able to contain her outrage any longer, the old doll blurted for all to hear:

"Shame! Smoking in public! . . . I would rather commit adultery than be seen smoking!"

"I would too, dearie," squelched the young thing. "But I've got only a half-hour for lunch."

One member of the hospital auxiliary remained unmarried. Each new meeting became more unbearable for the poor woman. Her married sisters teased and kidded her mercilessly.

"But, Stella, darling," said one of them for the thousandth time, "you really should get married. Why don't you find a husband?"

Exasperated, she got up. "Girls, may I have your attention, please? I am not looking for a husband, I LIKE being single . . . I do not wish to get married. Please do not mention this subject again. Here are my reasons: I have a fireplace that smokes, a dog that growls, a parrot that won't talk to me, a cat that stays out 'til three in the morning . . . what do I want with a husband?"

The matter was not mentioned again.

"George says I look like a million."
"Every year of it, sweetie."

"Hi, girls, see my new mink? How do I look?"
"Guilty."

"She'll never make *Who's Who,* but if anyone ever comes up with a *What's That. . . .*"

72

Frank Case, Algonquin Hotel manager, on a certain lady: "When you ask her a question, it's like taking your finger out of the dike."

"... The street is full of humiliations of the proud...."
—RALPH WALDO EMERSON

The great producer-director, George S. Kaufman, for more than thirty years entertained America with success after success on the Broadway stage. During those thirty years he delighted his intimates with his sharp and sometimes cutting wit.

Seated in a theater beside a woman who chattered incessantly, Kaufman said finally: "Madam, have you no UNEXPRESSED thoughts?"

He scoffed at theories about "art" in the theater. Actress Ruth Gordon once raved to him about a script.

"There's no scenery at all," she explained. "The audience has to IMAGINE I'm eating dinner in a crowded restaurant. Then, in Scene Two, the audience IMAGINES I'm home in my dressing room."

"And the second night," said Kaufman, "YOU have to imagine there's an audience."

When he wrote the Marx Brothers' comedy, *The Coconuts,* he got into an argument with Groucho over a joke.

To justify his stand, Groucho said facetiously: "Don't forget, they laughed at Fulton and his steamboat."

"Not at matinees," snapped Kaufman.

He once told a snob that he traced his own ancestry (Jewish), back to Sir Roderick Kaufman, who went on the Crusades—as a spy, of course, added Kaufman.

A week after attending a farewell dinner for a writer who was going to Hollywood, he saw the writer, still in New York.

"Ah," George observed, "forgotten, but not gone."

Though normally the most considerate of directors, guiding the players in a hushed whisper as if asking their advice, Kaufman did not take kindly to any tampering with his lines. During the run of *First Lady,* he went to Florida on a vacation. When he returned, he found that the leading lady had changed a number of his lines. He sent her the following wire:

YOUR PERFORMANCE MAGNIFICENT AND IMPROVING DAILY. SORRY I CAN'T SAY THE SAME FOR SOME OF YOUR LINES.

It was amateur night at the neighborhood theater. Sometimes, big-name entertainers and producers would drop in to see if there were any potential stars among the amateurs.

One night, a young amateur impersonator was well into his act when he noticed Frankie Laine sitting in the audience. He immediately switched his act into a high-gear imitation of Mr. Laine. After the show was over, our young friend immediately sought out Frankie in the lobby and asked:

"You saw and heard my impression of you. What do you think?"

"Well," said Laine, "I think one of us is pretty lousy!"

It was Charles Dickens who quipped about an unpleasant woman:

"She still aims at youth . . . though she shot by it years ago."

Will Rogers, the newspaperman–philosopher–cowboy, covered several Presidential campaigns in the 20's and 30's. One young reporter who idolized Rogers, but pestered him constantly, suggested:

"Mr. Rogers, I'm covering strictly the serious side of the convention. If I see anything funny, I'll let you know."

"That's fine, son," agreed Rogers. "And if I see anything serious, I'll let *you* know."

Toulouse Lautrec, outraged at overhearing a woman referring to a painting of his as "filthy," could not contain himself. The painting portrayed a partially clad woman and a man. The gallery visitor had commented how horrible and immoral it was to display in a public place a piece of art portraying a disgusting woman undressing in front of a man.

Lautrec, slightly drunk and outraged by her comment, bellowed at her: "Madam, that lady is dressing, not undressing. The gentleman is her husband. They are about to celebrate their twenty-fifth wedding anniversary. They will be spending the evening with their son. He is a taxidermist. I am appalled, madam, by your attitude.

"You have maligned these people. It only goes to prove what I have always said, evil is in the eyes of the beholder . . . I'll thank you not to look at my pictures!"

And so saying . . . he left the gallery.

Here's a gentle wipeout reported by Florabel Muir in the *New York Daily News*:

"The late Cardinal Spellman was much beloved by those in the entertainment world who knew him. Bob

Hope was reminiscing about one of their overseas meetings.

" 'I attended his midnight mass for the troops in Viet Nam,' says Hope. 'I was dead tired and fell asleep, so the next morning I called on the Cardinal to offer my apologies.'

" 'That's all right, Bob,' said the Cardinal. 'I once saw your show at Loew's State and now we're even.' "

Will Jones reported this one in the *Minneapolis Tribune*:

"Orson Welles was showing the pilot film for a proposed Welles TV series to the program chief of one of the networks.

" 'I like it, Orson,' said the executive. 'But will the average jerk understand it?'

" 'Well,' said Welles, 'YOU understood it.' "

Bob Hope claims General Westmoreland put him down during his trip to Viet Nam to entertain the troops.

Says Bob: "He always kept a chicken around the house in case I needed a blood transfusion."

During World War II, General Montgomery, in the African campaign, finished a briefing of his officers before sending them off to battle Rommel's army with:

". . . And remember, gentlemen, God is on our side!"

After a brief silence, a junior officer side-mouthed under his breath:

"Yeah? In support or in command?"

Eugene O'Neill, while on a cruise, was once ordered off the captain's deck by one of the hands.

"This is the captain's bridge, sir. Sorry, you'll have to leave," explained the young sailor.

"Sir," said O'Neill. "You are talking to the world's greatest playwright."

"I'm sorry, Mr. Shaw, I still can't allow you to stay here."

Most famous people receive, surely, many letters and photographs from people convinced they are look-alikes. Mark Twain was no exception. He reportedly was deluged with a couple of hundred of these annually. He finally got tired of it and had a form letter drawn up which he mailed out on receipt of each new twin. The letter read:

> My Dear Sir:
>
> I thank you very much for your letter and the photograph. In my opinion, you are more like me than any of my other doubles. I may even say that you resemble me more than I do myself. In fact I intend to use your picture to shave by.
>
> > Yours thankfully,
> >
> > Samuel Clemens

The *Toronto Telegram*'s Bob Blackburn, reviewing Phyllis Diller's appearance at the O'Keefe Center: ". . . And speaking of shape, this girl is like Jayne Mansfield, Sophia Loren, and Anita Ekberg all in one—all in one potato sack, that is."

When James. J. Corbett was heavyweight champion of the world, he took his old dad to visit Steve Brodie at his famous saloon in the lower Bowery. Corbett wanted his father to shake the hand of the man who had gained fame for his spectacular leap from the Brooklyn Bridge.

"I'm very proud to make your acquaintance," said the old man. "I'm happy to shake the hand of the man who jumped over the Brooklyn Bridge."

"He didn't jump *over* the Brooklyn Bridge, Father," corrected the younger Corbett. "He jumped *off* it."

"Shucks," grunted the old man, turning to leave. "I thought he jumped over it. Any damn fool can jump *off* it."

Phyllis Diller to starlet:
"You've got the same problem I have, honey. The only difference between you and Sophia Loren is that you're regular screen and she's cinemascope."

Pierre Elliott Trudeau, Canada's "swinger" Prime Minister, quickly established himself, even before capturing the Liberal leadership in March of 1968, as potentially one of the great wipeout artists of his decade.

Trudeau is in his forties, a bachelor, a millionaire, and is in many ways unorthodox. He will, perhaps, have to adjust a little. The dignity of the Prime Minister's office and his colleagues will demand a more conventional approach to dress and automobiles.

During his campaign for the leadership of the Liberal party, the press made much of his "swinging, almost mod" approach. For the fifth tedious time in successive press conferences he had been asked by a youthful news reporter whether, if he attained Canada's highest office, he would "get rid of his Mercedes."

"Would I get rid of my Mercedes?" asked Trudeau. "Well, that all depends on whether you mean the car or the girl."

Time Magazine reported that Trudeau gained Cabinet Minister Walter Gordon's endorsement for the Liberal leadership in spite of the fact that in answer to Gordon's resignation based on the difficulty of limiting foreign investment (U.S.) and capital in the Canadian economy, Trudeau quipped:

"It's very easy to get rid of foreign capital, *mon cher ami*. Castro did it in three weeks!"

Bruce Taylor in the *Montreal Star* reports this Pierre Elliott Trudeau wipeout. (I've also seen this same one credited to Shaw and Churchill.)

"At one of Prime Minister Trudeau's meetings the other day," Taylor reports, "a frustrated female civil servant, trying to get a rise out of him with her heckling, finally shouted:

" 'If I were married to you, I'd put arsenic in your coffee.'

"To which he retorted: 'And if I were your husband, madame, I'd drink it.' "

Li'l Abner's creator, Al Capp, was at a cocktail party at the Mayflower Hotel in Washington. One of the guests was Harry S Truman, then President. Capp was presented to Mr. Truman as "Al Capp, the comic strip creator."

"Oh?" asked the President. "Which comic strip?"

Mr. Truman was then introduced to Capp as the President.

"Oh?" snapped Capp. "Which country?"

Sinclair Lewis to a pest who had asked him a dozen times why he never portrayed a happy husband in his stories:

"For the same reason, madam, that I have never portrayed a five-footed elephant that could fly."

Any politician who can duck a reporter's question and leave the newsman satisfied, has a place in the hearts of all putdownophiles. Canada's young bachelor Prime Minister Trudeau satisfied this group.

Before Canada's last federal election, Trudeau, at a

press conference, was asked to clarify his stand on Viet Nam.

"Are you a hawk or a dove?" asked a newsman.

"Neither," shot back Trudeau. "I'm a chicken hawk."

Dave Harriman, at the C.B.C. in Toronto, tells this one:

A loud-mouth, name-dropping junior exec took his secretary to a swank club in Toronto. She was impressed. A couple of tables away sat *Bonanza* star, Lorne Greene, in town for some special shows. Our boy figured, here's a great chance to impress his secretary with all the celebrities he knows. So, when she got up to go and powder her nose, he went over to Mr. Greene and said:

"You don't know me, but this is my secretary's birthday, and I wonder if when she gets back you couldn't just come over and put your arm around my shoulder and say hello, just as if we were old friends. She doesn't get out much and she'd really be thrilled by that, and it'll impress her no end."

Good-natured Lorne agreed.

A half-hour later, the couple were sitting over their dessert when Lorne Greene, Pa Cartwright himself, came over and slapped our friend on the back and said:

"Hi there, you old son of a gun. . . . How're ya doin'?"

Our friend turned to him . . . looked at him for a moment, and said: "Look, Lorne, why do you keep bugging me? How many times have I told you, leave me alone? Now blow!"

Andrew Carnegie was once visited by a socialist who eloquently preached to him the injustice of one man possessing so much money. He proposed a more equitable distribution of wealth.

Carnegie cut the matter short by asking his secretary for a generalized statement of his many possessions and holdings, at the same time looking up the figures on world population in his almanac. He figured for a moment on his desk pad and then instructed his secretary:

"Give the man sixteen cents. That's his share of my wealth."

John Randolph and Henry Clay once had an argument in the Senate. It was such an angry quarrel that they did not speak to each other afterward for quite awhile.

One day they met on Pennsylvania Avenue where the sidewalk was very narrow. As Randolph came up, he looked Henry Clay in the eye, and, not moving an inch from the sidewalk, hissed:

"I never turn out for scoundrels."

"I *always* do," said Mr. Clay, as he stepped politely off the walk and let Randolph pass.

One of history's most amazing men, Thomas Edison, who was granted more than a thousand patents for his marvelous inventions, was, naturally, a very busy man. He intensely disliked formal affairs, which to him were always stuffy and boring.

At one ghastly, dull gathering he decided to try and slip away unnoticed to his lab and get back to the work he so dearly loved. As he was lounging near the doorway waiting for the right moment to make his escape, his host came up to him.

"It's so good to see you here at our little gathering, Mr. Edison. We're honored to have such a great inventor in our midst. By the way, what are you working on now?"

"My exit," sighed Edison, and made it.

A putdown that *could have* happened:

Late that great night, after months of toil in his lab, Thomas Edison succeeds. He connects the wires and the incandescent electric light glows! What joy!

Mrs. Edison shouts at him from upstairs:

"Tom, it's three A.M.! Turn off that damn light and come to bed! . . ."

Mark Twain was a bad one. He put 'em down every chance he had.

He was once cornered by a chap who loved to impress everyone by spouting statistics that no one really cared much about.

"Do you realize," he lapeled Twain, "that every time I breathe, somebody somewhere in the world dies? Isn't that amazing?"

"Yes, it is," snapped Twain. "Have you tried chewing cloves?"

A businessman, whose ethics were suspect, once told Twain:

"Before I die, I mean to make a pilgrimage to the Holy Land. I will climb to the top of Mount Sinai and read the Ten Commandments aloud."

"I have a better idea," said Twain. "Why don't you stay here and keep them?"

When Oswald's bullets felled John F. Kennedy that day in Dallas, we lost not just a politician, humanitarian, statesman, and great president, but also a humorist with a very sharp and, if necessary, crushing wit.

During his campaign against Nixon, he once observed:

"Mr. Nixon, like the rest of us, has had his troubles in this campaign. At one point even the *Wall Street Journal* was criticizing his tactics. That is like the *Osservatore Romano* criticizing the Pope."

Again on Nixon: "I wonder, when he put his finger under Mr. Khrushchev's nose, whether he was saying: 'I know you are ahead of us in rockets, Mr. Khrushchev, but we are ahead of you in color television.'

"Personally, I would just as soon look at black and white television and be ahead of them in rockets."

At a press conference, answering criticism on the appointment of Robert Kennedy as Attorney General of the U.S.A.:

"Many among you feel he is too young for the job. Well, I feel there is nothing wrong with giving Robert some experience as Attorney General before he goes out to practice law."

During his campaign against Nixon, the press made much ado about Nixon's experience and know-how because of his tenure as Vice President under Eisenhower. John Kennedy quashed his critics with these words at a press conference:

"Gentlemen, I know a banker who served thirty years as president of a bank. He had more experience, 'til his bank went broke, than any other banker in Massachusetts.

"If I ever go into the banking business, I do not plan to hire him . . . and he knows the business from top to bottom."

For reasons that will be obvious, we cannot use the names of the participants in this real drama that took place somewhere in New York at a typical celebrity-studded cocktail bash.

A very well-known homosexual was being taunted by a TV actor, suspiciously proud of his own masculinity. Words passed between the two 'til the actor shouted at the homosexual: "You wouldn't know what to do with a * * * * [female organ] if you saw one!"

"Yes, I would," shot back our friend. "I would take a broom and kill it!"

Sometimes Jack E. Leonard says it so fast, you're not even sure you've been put down. It SOUNDS like you've been squelched and usually you have been.

Elizabeth Taylor was being honored at a dinner one night in New York. Jack E. Leonard was a head-table guest.

The M. C. jokingly opened the evening by saying: "Tonight, we present the loves and lives of Elizabeth Taylor."

Leonard interrupted with: "Relax, folks, we're gonna be here a long time."

During a televised Friar's dinner honoring Ed Sullivan about fifteen years ago, the toastmaster said something like: "We are here tonight to heap our love and affection on a man of many virtues."

Leonard burst in with: "Yeah, name two!"

The late and many-wived Alexander King, who appeared as a semi-regular on the Jack Paar Show, was once put down by an amateur . . . which was rare. Jack's first guest that night was a market-research expert who specialized in teen-agers. He went on at some length about teen-agers and their motivations in buying and the kinds of products the teeny-boppers were spending their money on.

Alexander King could take no more. "Never have I heard such slush, such drivel. How can you, sir, dedicate yourself to researching something as useless and trashy as the likes and dislikes of teen-agers?"

Unhesitatingly, the analyst shot back: "I just analyze them, Mr. King . . . I don't marry them."

Oscar Levant to George Gershwin: "George, if you had it to do all over, would you fall in love with yourself again?"

Commenting on the Dinah Shore TV show years ago, Levant quipped: "My doctor won't allow me to watch her show, I'm a diabetic."

Mickey Rooney: "Of course I'm a Jack Paar fan. Once I stayed up until I couldn't sleep anymore."

A Hollywood starlet meets another in a posh restaurant. Neither beauty is very fond of the other. "Darling, how nice to see you. I'm so glad I ran into you today, I have marvelous news. I've just been offered $25,000 to stay in Hollywood. Isn't that wonderful?"

"It certainly is," said her *friend*. "Who made the offer, New York?"

An oft-married starlet at cocktail party: "I'm getting married again."

"Oh, is it anyone you know?"

It was intermission. Two playwrights met in the lobby of the theater where one of them had a play being performed.

"I hear you're not doing anything much this year," said the employed author. "Well, that's the way it is some years, I guess. Still, you must admit, you're not the best. By the way, how did you happen to come to my play tonight?"

"I went to see the doctor this afternoon, I have a bad cold. He told me to avoid crowds."

Don Rickles to TV personality in audience: "Hey! There's Robert Barton, the TV host, ladies and gentlemen. Hi, Bob. Caught your show yesterday. . . . Anything you do after that is a comeback."

Announcer on CFCF Radio, Montreal: ". . . And that was Derek Lind reporting the news. Thanks, Derek. You've never sounded better . . . which is very sad when you think about it."

An out-of-work actor was approached for the eleventh time about his overdue rent. "I wish you wouldn't bug me about the rent. Don't you realize, some day they'll point to this room and say George Roberts slept here?"

"If I don't get the rent by eleven tonight, they'll be able to say it tomorrow."

Even in Hollywood, where titanic egos are generally tolerated and even fed, patience with the melon-heads sometimes expires.

There's a classic story about an aging actor who had become unbearable as he grew in stature in the motion-picture business. He met his Waterloo and was destroyed by nine little words from a cameraman.

"Goddamn you!" he yelled at the cameraman. "How many times have I told you, you're not photographing my best side! You're not photographing my best side!"

A hush fell on the set. The crew waited for the answer that must come.

"I *can't* photograph your best side," offered the cameraman.

"And why not?"

"BECAUSE YOU'RE ALWAYS SITTING ON IT . . . *THAT'S* WHY," he screamed.

A comedian, referring to a competitor at the next table:

"Comic? . . . Some comic! He couldn't ad lib a burp at a Hungarian picnic."

Two starlets discussing their box office:

"Listen, the last time I made a personal appearance at the Bijou I drew a line four blocks long."

"And did they make you erase it?"

Noel Coward to severely dressed author and playwright Edna Ferber: "Why, Edna, you look almost like a man."

"So," Miss Ferber said, "do you."

". . . The Mets 'A' team played the Mets 'B' team. Both lost."
     —BOB SYLVESTER

Coach Punch Imlach of the Toronto Maple Leafs' hockey club told this story at a Rotary luncheon:

Two of his nephews were visiting him one day. They were both trying out for their Little League teams at school. Punch asked one of the lads what position he was playing. The lad replied that he was playing left-wing.

"And what position does your brother play?" asked Imlach.

"Oh, he doesn't play any position," answered the kid.

"Why not?"

"Well," the peewee went on, "he can't skate, can't pass, can't check, and can't remember the rules. All he can do is shoot his mouth off all the time."

"So what happened?" asked the famous man.

"They made him coach," explained the boy.

Tex Coulter, former Montreal Alouette great, unhappy with several decisions by a football official, called on him in his dressing room after the game. He suggested that perhaps they could locate the RCF's rule book and check out a few of the referee's decisions.

"I carry my rule book with me at all times, Tex," said the official.

"Well," drawled Tex, "I wonder would y'all mind me havin' a look at it?"

"Why not?" said our friend and produced the rule book out of his back pocket.

Tex took the book, leafed through it for a moment, studied a page here and there, handed it back to the referee, saying:

"Thank yuh, ah jest wanted tuh see if it was printed in Braille!"

Yogi Berra, exchanging insults with an umpire: "Yeah? Is that right? Yeah? Just tell me one thing, buster . . . how do you get that square head into that round mask?"

It takes yards of guts to put down several tons of men. . . .

Sports commentator Tom Harvin in *Quote* Magazine tells about the time the Notre Dame team slumped into the locker room at the half, expecting a rousing chewing-out from their renowned coach, Knute Rockne.

The score was disastrous. But the Rock said nothing, and a depressed silence filled the room until an official announced two minutes to game time. Then, Rockne said quietly and wearily: "Okay, let's go, girls."

An aroused Irish team stormed onto the field and won the game.

"Hey, Hon. The golf pro at the club says I play a lot like Palmer."

"Yeah? . . . Betsy or Arnold?"

A certain ballplayer, who felt an umpire had made several bad calls on him during the game, happened to run into that very umpire that evening. The official was eating with some friends in a restaurant and suggested our friend join him, which he did.

"No hard feelings about this afternoon, eh, Bill?" asked the Ump. "I know you thought some of the calls I made out there were wrong."

" 'Course there are no hard feelings, George," said the ball player. "And just to prove it, let me tell your friends a good story I heard just an hour ago. It goes like this:

"The devil kept challenging St. Peter to a baseball game and St. Peter kept refusing. But one day a great calamity hit earth and the Giants and Dodgers and Yankees all went to heaven. St. Peter figures this would be a pretty safe time to accept Satan's offer of a ball game.

"He called up the devil on the hot line and said: 'Okay, Satan baby, you're on. Name the time and place.'

" 'I know what you're up to, Pete,' said Satan. 'But you'll still lose.'

" 'How can I lose?' asked S. P., 'I've got all the great ball players.'

" 'I know,' said Satan. 'But I've got all the umpires.' "

"Look," the golfer screamed at his caddy, "if you don't keep your big mouth shut, you'll drive me out of my mind."

"That's no drive, mister," squelched the caddy. "That's a putt."

Caddy: "Let me say this about your game, mister. I wouldn't say you were the WORST golfer I have ever seen on this course, but I've seen places today that I've never seen before."

Wipeout sign note in Omaha: THE OAKLAND ATH-LETICS AREN'T VERY.

94

Sometimes you can prevent a wipeout by getting in the first word . . . put *yourself* down, it's less embarrassing.

The over-confident golfer teed up on the first hole, took a look at the fairway, and announced to the gallery of on-lookers that he thought this would be about a two-stroke hole. "One good drive and a putt should do it." He took a swing, topped the ball badly, and it dribbled off the first tee about four yards.

This is where somebody puts you down, right?

Not if you move fast enough. What did our friend do? He walked straight over to the ball, took his stance, and announced: "Now for one helluva putt!"

"Caddy, why do you keep looking at your watch?"
"This isn't a watch, sir, it's a compass."

"I'd move heaven and earth to break my 110 score."
"Try moving heaven, Bill," said his partner. "You've already moved plenty of earth today."

"Caddy, why didn't you see where that ball went?"
"Well, it doesn't usually go anywhere, Mister Gaunt. You got me off guard."

"Well, did you think I looked better today, caddy?"
"Yessir, those new golf pants make you look much better."

"What kind of game did he have? What kind of a golfer is he? Madam, he lost a ball in the washer."

"I lost a brand new ball today."
"Oh, did the string break?"

"He's the only guy in the world who has an unplayable lie when he tees up."

"This looks like a tricky hole, boy. What do you think I should use?"
"An old ball, sir."

"The doctor says I can't play golf."
"Ah, he's played with you too, huh?"

"I've figured out a way to take ten strokes off every game."
"You bought an eraser?"

"You must be the world's worst caddy."
"No, sir, that would be too much of a coincidence."

"You're improving, George. The ball trembled that time."

"What'll I do with this, caddy?" asked the player, holding up a foot-long divot he had plowed out of the turf.
"Why not take it home and practice on it, sir?"

"How would you have played that last shot, caddy?"
"Under an assumed name."

". . . War has resulted in fiction that is divisible into three parts—neurotic, erotic, and tommy-rotic. . . ."
    —DAVID RAMER

There's a famous World War II story. In its telling and re-telling over the years, the ship and victim have lost their identities.

The ship's captain, enraged at having to repeat his commands three times over, grabbed the speaking tube from the hands of one of the ship's officers and roared into it:

"Is there a blithering idiot at the end of this tube?"

Back came the immediate reply: "Not at THIS end, sir!"

In the army, drill-sergeants are not generally considered to be the most loved people. There was one particularly bad egg in Fort Dix who had been tormenting and badgering his men mercilessly for weeks.

The day finally came when the drill-training period was over, and it was time for the recruits to move on to more constructive activities. Most of the recruits were appalled when it became evident that one of the men was taking up a collection to buy the sergeant a gift before the men moved on. It was to be a kind of good-bye token.

Contributions poured in, however, when it was realized

what kind of gift the men would be giving the good sergeant. A beautifully framed portrait of Lassie, inscribed: "With love, from Mother."

A squad of cadets had been out on the rifle range for their first try at marksmanship. They knelt at 250 yards and fired. Not a hit. They moved up to 200 yards and fired. Not a hit. Finally, they were moved by the exasperated sergeant to 100 yards.

"Fire!" he roared.

Every cadet missed the target.

"Tenshun!" he barked. "Fix bayonets! Charge! It's your only chance!"

"Sarge, do you think they'll send me overseas?"
"Only if we're invaded."

A Russian army officer hounded an American reporter in Moscow for weeks about his negative reporting on the Soviet armed forces.

"You never have anything good to say about us," he complained. "Always, you pick little faults. The Soviet army is the most democratic army in the world. Do you realize something? I just received an order from headquarters that banishes forever the class-system practice of dining in separate quarters. From now on the officers and men eat together, like comrades should . . . in the same dining room."

The American reporter agreed that that indeed was a newsworthy story and would definitely be printed in his paper.

A week later the Russian received a clipping of the story in the mail. It was a very brief item under the huge headline: SOVIET OFFICERS ORDERED TO EAT WITH THEIR PRIVATES.

Barber to new recruit: "Hey, soldier, wanna keep your sideburns?"

"Sure."

"Catch."

"Anybody in this hut know shorthand?" asked the sergeant.

Six recruits, smelling an easy detail, immediately volunteered.

"Okay, you six, get over to the mess hall right away. They're shorthanded."

"Soldier," asked the lieutenant, "do you have change for a dollar?"

"Sure, buddy."

"That's no way to address an officer," screamed the lieutenant. "Now let's try that again. . . . Soldier, do you have change for a dollar?"

"No, sir!"

A class of G.I.s—all potential sergeants—was listening to a particularly boring lecture by the sergeant who was currently making life miserable for them.

"A good sergeant," he said, "can't be made. . . . A good sergeant has to be born. . . . Any questions?"

"Yeah, sarge. Is that in or out of wedlock?"

He was the roughest, toughest, most demanding and hated colonel in the army. He suffered a humiliating Waterloo one day during inspection.

He marched up and down the ranks, his eyes searching for a slip somewhere. He stopped in front of a young private, stared at him long and hard, put his face up to the kid's nose, and yelled:

"Soldier, straighten that tie!"

"You want me to straighten the tie right now, Colonel?" asked the soldier.

"Yes," boomed the colonel. "Right now."

The young lad then broke his stance, quietly laid his rifle on the ground, reached over, and straightened the colonel's tie.

A marine regiment arrived back at the base after a long tough tour at the front. The colonel discovered, much to his alarm, that a contingent of WACs was on the base and would remain there until orders came through assigning them to various posts and duties. Now, remember that these men had been at the front a long time and hadn't even seen a woman for two months! The colonel was justifiably very concerned. He stormed into the quarters of the WAC's commanding officer and demanded that the girls either be taken off the base immediately or else kept locked up for the duration of their stay.

"How dare you make such an idiotic suggestion?" the C.O. cried. "Lock them up indeed! You can be sure there'll be no trouble." Tapping her forehead, she added: "My girls have it up here."

"Madam," he roared. "It makes no difference where your girls have it. My boys will find it."

A young man in a beautifully cut silk suit swaggers into a recruiting office to enlist. (The story is already suspect . . . right?) He impatiently answers the questions put to him by the recruiting clerk.

"Did you go to elementary school?" the clerk asked.

"Did I go to elementary school? . . . Are you joking, sir? . . . I attended Harvard, Yale, I have my B.A., M.A., Ph.D., studied political science in Paris, London, and Vienna. I studied economics under Professor Rheinhart in Prague for four years and taught for two years at the University of Lichtenstein. What do you think of *that,* sir?"

The clerk wearily reached for a large rubber stamp and with great force stamped the recruit's application with a big LITERATE.

"Hello. This is the Canadian Armed Forces Depot."

"Hello. We need twelve vehicles in the parade square immediately, two of them must be limousines."

"What are the limousines for? To haul those fat-slob generals around in, I bet."

"Soldier, do you know who this is speaking?"

"No, I don't."

"This is General Walker at this end."

"Do you know who this is speaking, sir?"

"No, I don't."

"See ya 'round . . . fatso."

American officer, concluding a lecture on world military history:

"And so that's why Napoleon always wore a red tunic. If he was wounded, the blood would not show through his uniform and his men would not know that he had been injured. Now, before we end this lecture, are there any questions?"

Young recruit: "Yessir, I have a question. Why do the officers in our army wear brown?"

". . . He looked at me as if I were a side dish he hadn't ordered. . . ."

Restaurants are great places to squash 'em. So many people, so many opportunities for a quick mind to grasp.

"Waiter, do you serve crabs in this dump?"
"Yes, sir, what'll you have?"

"How is the soup, sir?"
"To tell you the truth, I'm sorry I stirred it."

"How did you find your steak, sir?"
"I just lifted one of the Brussels sprouts and there it was."

"Waiter, there's a dead fly in my soup."
"Yes, it's the boilin' wot kills 'em, sir."

Grouchy customer: "Waiter? What time is it?"
"Sorry, sir, this isn't my table."

Noisy customer in a very elegant restaurant puts a napkin around his neck. The maitre d' is aghast. This just isn't done. Did he handle it beautifully?

He walked up to our bibbed slob and asked, in front of a tableful of his friends: "Shave or haircut, m'sieu?"

"What can I have, waiter?"

"Everything's on the menu, sir."

"Yes, I can see that. Would you bring me a clean one, please?"

"Do you like our renovations, monsieur? We are now a first-class restaurant."

"Yes, I like it except for one thing, Pierre."

"What is that, m'sieu?"

"The monogram on my napkin just crawled away."

The diner had sent the waitress scurrying back and forth. He was not to be easily satisfied. By the time he and his friends had finished their meal, she was completely exhausted.

Came time to pay the check and the victim left four nickels for the waitress. She looked at the coins and smiled.

"Before you and your friends leave, sir, perhaps you might be interested in having a character reading. I can tell fortunes from coins."

Our friend lunged at the bait. "That would be lovely . . . thank you, miss."

"I'll just use these coins you've left on the table, sir. Now let's see. I can tell by this first coin that you are quite well off."

He agreed that: "He wasn't doin' too bad."

"I can see by this second nickel that you were born here and live alone."

"Right again," he said.

"I can see by this third nickel that you're not married."

"Right."

"And," she squelched, "I can see by this last nickel, that your father wasn't married either."

"Waiter, what do I do in this lousy restaurant to get some water?"

"You might try setting yourself on fire, sir."

The scene is a posh Chinese restaurant. Harvey is impressing his best girl. He decides to put on the Chinese waiter bit.

"Ah . . . Chollie . . . bling me some flied lice . . . okay?"

"Okay," said the waiter. "But are you really having trouble pronouncing fried rice, or are you being a bit of a plick?"

"This is the worst service I ever experienced, waiter . . . you're not fit to serve a pig!"

"I really am trying to be, sir."

"Waiter, I see you serve blended coffee here."

"Blended coffee, sir?"

"Yes, yesterday's and today's."

"Maitre d', just as a matter of curiosity . . . the waiter that took our order . . . did he leave any family?"

Here's a "what-have-I-got-to-lose, I'm-quitting-today-anyway" putdown.

The waiter in this little drama is on his last day, having quit that morning to escape a tyrannical boss. A customer comes in.

"Waiter, would you ask the orchestra to play *Moon River*, please?"

"I'm sorry, sir, they'll be playing that tune during their midnight set."

"But I won't be here at midnight."

"Sir, may I ask what you will be ordering?"

"Steak."

"You'll be here at midnight."

The oft-quoted Harry Miller in Bruce Taylor's *Montreal Star* column tells what he swears he overheard in a Montreal eatery. If true, it's one of the best:

The waitress brings our hero an unusually small portion of roast beef. He looks at it for a moment and says:

"Right! That's exactly what I want . . . bring me some of that."

There is a small town in Ohio which boasts all of two restaurants, only one of which remains open on Sundays. Not really much choice for the bachelors of the community.

In walked a weary, resigned, hungry man for his usual Sunday dinner. He stared at the worn old menu that he had looked at a thousand times before, slowly looked up at the waitress, and asked:

"Don't you have anything that'll effect acute heartburn immediately instead of at two-thirty tomorrow morning?"

A lovely steered her cheapie boyfriend into a posh restaurant. They dined luxuriously. After an elegant dinner, while sipping her third Grand Marnier she said:

"Darling, you look ill. Is it something I ate?"

"Waiter, I must say, I don't like all these flies in my soup."

"Show me which ones you don't like, sir, and I'll get rid of them for you."

"May I help you with the soup, sir?"

"Just what do you mean by that remark?"

"Well, from the sound of things, we thought you might need to be dragged ashore."

Boss, complaining to waitress:

"You're hopeless. Each week you break more things than your wages amount to. I don't know how to solve that problem."

"Why not give me a raise?"

"Look, Jim, why are you always trying to impress me? So you spoke to the waiter in French. So big deal. So what good is it to know French? What did he tell you, waiter?"

"He told me to give you the check, sir."

"Excuse me, are you the manager of this pub?"

"Why, yes, I am ... can I help you?"

"Yes, I was wondering how many barrels of beer you sell here every week?"

"Oh, we average about forty barrels or so, why?"

"Well, how would you like to sell eighty barrels a week."

"Love to. How do I do that?"

"By filling up the glasses."

"... She had a lot of fat that did not fit...."
    —H. G. WELLS

Fat people get it. Skinny ones don't. A skinny person is kidded, but gently. A fat person gets it everyday right between the layers.

Fat wipeouts generally are one liners . . . devastatingly hurtful. They all open with the same first line:

"I don't want to say she's fat, but:

"She has to jack her legs apart to get her slacks on."

"She can get to Vancouver just by rolling over three times."

"When she hiccups in a bathing suit, it starts a ripple like somebody adjusting a venetian blind."

"She's been elected governor of the National Girl Stout Movement."

"She puts her makeup on with a paint roller."

"She's fat in places where other girls don't even have places."

"She uses a hammock for a chin strap."

"She needs a bookmark to find her pearls."

"She had to let the shower curtain out."

"She's America's fastest growing sport."

"She has a shadow at high noon."

"She has the Jackie look. Jackie Gleason."

"She had to buy longer shoe laces."

"When she got married, they threw puffed rice."

"She hung up her stocking at Christmas and Santa left a bedroom suite in it."

"She had mumps for five days and no one knew it."

"She stepped on a penny scale and out came a card saying: COME BACK LATER, ALONE."

"She wears inner tubes for garters."

"Five minutes after the music stops, she's still shimmying."

"She's on the critical list at Vic Tanny's."

"She weighs about a hundred and plenty."

". . . A prejudice is a vagrant opinion without visible means of support. . . ."
—AMBROSE BIERCE

Although we often find the "hate" jokes nauseating in their implied attacks on a specific race or nationality, it can't be argued that they are not funny or that they do not have a place in a wipeout collection. For, indeed, they are putdowns of the most intense kind.

They're based on the "did-you-hear-about-the-little-moron" jokes we used to tell as children. They've since graduated to the sickies that have been popular for about ten years.

In the U.S.A. they are directed against Poles, Negroes, Italians, and Irish. In Canada, the victim is the Newfoundlander or the French-Canadian. In eastern Europe, obviously, it's the Russian or the gypsy.

The insults are not justifiably applied to any group, but in the cold, cruel world of the wipeout, SOMEBODY has to be a victim.

There are hundreds of genetic putdowns, funny to almost everyone but the victim. We list, for the record, a group we found to be a degree above the straight hate insults. Our victims? *The Yougarians.*

Did you hear about the Yougarian orchestra that stopped in the middle of a performance to clean the saliva out of their instruments? What's wrong with that? This was a string orchestra.

The perfect gift for a Yougarian who has everything? A garbage truck to keep it in.

Why don't Yougarians kill flies? They're the national bird of Yougaria.

What rides on a white pig and wears thongs and white robes? Lawrence of Yougaria.

Do you know why it takes a Yougarian five days to wash his basement windows?
He needs four and a half days to dig the holes for the ladder.

Did you hear about the Yougarian race driver at Indianapolis who came in last? His average speed, 4.5 miles per hour. He had to make 75 pit stops. Three for fuel, 2 to have tires changed, and 70 to ask directions.

Did you hear about the proposed largest zoo in the world? The UN is planning to put a fence around the capital of Yougaria.

The Yougarian bride? She wore something old, something new, something borrowed, something blue, something orange, something lilac, something chartreuse, something red, something yellow, something black, something green. . . .

Did you hear about the posh Yougarian wedding? It was really posh. The bride's veil practically covered her slacks.

Sign on a Yougarian garbage truck: WE CATER WEDDINGS.

He had a great job in Yougaria. Rode shotgun on a garbage truck.

What's the capital of Yougaria? About seventeen dollars.

How did the Yougarian get all those holes in his forehead? Learning to eat with a fork.

A Yougarian marriage proposal: "You're gonna have a what?"

How can you tell a Yougarian funeral? All the garbage trucks have their lights on.

Did you hear about the Yougarian beauty contest? Nobody won.

"Do you know how to save a Yougarian?"
"No."
"That's good."

Gross Ignorance: 144 Yougarians.

What's the best way to grease a Ferrari? Run over a Yougarian.

What do you get when you cross a midget with a Yougarian? A short garbageman.

What's the difference between a Yougarian grandmother and an elephant?
About seven pounds.

Dope Ring? That's twelve Yougarians sitting in a circle.

A Yougarian car pool. Eight Yougarians carrying a Volkswagen to work.

The Yougarian who had a pair of water skis that he never got to use. Couldn't find a lake on a hill.

You know what XXX is, don't you? That's three Yougarians co-signing a note.

Why doesn't General Motors give their Yougarian mechanics a coffee break?
Takes too long to re-train them.

You heard about the Yougarian who wouldn't go out with his wife because he found out she's married?

". . . They stood before the altar and supplied the fire themselves in which their fat was fried."

—AMBROSE BIERCE

I'm convinced that the soaring North American divorce rate is due largely to overdoses of togetherness. Dr. Norman Vincent Peale might go into a crouch with his blade switched on when he reads this, but many counselors and psychiatrists are now preaching that periods of "apartness" can be very healthy.

Girls, don't drag the old man with you everywhere. He might revert to his "primitive" instincts and punch you a lot about the head and shoulders. Or, he might grasp an opportunity to put you down so hard, they'll need a putty knife to scrape your ego off the tile.

One of Canada's great radio men, Bill Brady, gives the following example, which he swears is true:

Once upon a time, in a small Ontario city in Canada, there lived a man and a shrew. They were very married. She insisted that he accompany her everywhere. Never was he to be out of her sight! Fridays were hell! Shopping from four 'til ten at night.

They made their twenty-sixth stop of the afternoon and were in a crowded ladies-wear store at a busy shopping center. She was rummaging through one of those bargain counters that was jammed with ladies' panties and bras. There were many women at the counter fighting to get one of the bargains, when his wife held up a very brief pair of ladies' panties and shouted across the counter to him:

"Hey . . . do you like these?"

He shouted back to her: "I sure do, baby, but do you think your husband will like them?"

Should a man put his wife and/or her mother down? Well, decide for yourself after reading the following true story reported in a major magazine. Bill Gates, of Montreal, Canada, toiled for weeks to form the Henpecked Husbands Club. He finally got a large group interested.

The wipeout?

His wife wouldn't let him join.

Well, now that we've all agreed it's okay, . . . try these:

Husband overheard at a party muttering to his wife:

"What did I say to offend you, dear? It might come in useful again sometime."

"So this is your wife, eh, Harry? Tell us, how did you meet her?"

"I didn't meet her . . . she overtook me!"

"How long have you two been married?" asked the friend.

"We've been happily married for seven years," answered the husband, adding, "seven out of sixteen ain't bad."

"Darling, tomorrow is our third anniversary. That calls for leather gifts, doesn't it?"

"Yes, I have an idea. Why don't we exchange leather gifts. I'll get you a handbag and you can cook me one of your steaks."

"Tomorrow is our twenty-fifth wedding anniversary, Herman. What do you suggest?"
"How about two minutes of silence?"

"Harvey, tomorrow is our tin anniversary."
"Yeah, five years of eatin' out of cans."

"Darling, this is the fifteenth anniversary of our wedding day."
"Seems like yesterday I married you. I wish tomorrow was our wedding day."
"You do?"
"Yeah, I'd call it off."

"Jim, were you really fishing last weekend like you said?"
"Of course, sweetie."
"Well, one of the bass you were after Saturday, phoned and left her number."

"George! Come quickly, a wild tiger has gone into mother's tent!"
"Well, he got himself into that mess, let him get out of it."

"Gee, George, I never have anything to do. Doesn't the Mafia have a ladies' auxiliary?"

"Honey, it says here in the paper that in a remote area of Chile, the women pay their men ten dollars each time they make love to them. That's too good a deal. I think I'll go live in Chile."

"Go ahead, I'd just love to see you live on twenty dollars a month."

"You didn't have to marry me."
"Well, we weren't so sure at the time, were we?"

"Honey, unlock the door. I'm sorry I'm so late."
Silence.
"Honey, if you don't unlock this door, I'm gonna run down the street yelling at the top of my voice: 'I slept with my wife before we were married!' "
"Do and I'll be right behind you screaming: 'And he wasn't the only one!' "

"Honey, would you say I'm built like a Greek god?"
"No, I'd say you were built more like a Greek restaurant."

Get revenge on a man after he's dead? ... Why not ... particularly if he's deserving of a posthumous wipeout:

A good-for-nothing lazy bum dies. His wife has him cremated and puts his ashes in an hour glass. Every hour she inverts the glass saying: "Work you bum! Work!"

"Sheep are such stupid animals. Don't you agree, George?"
"Yes, my lamb."

"Do you think I'm as pretty as I was twenty years ago?"
"Sure ... it just takes you longer, that's all."

Wife, doing crossword: "Who was stronger than Samson, wiser than Solomon, wittier than Myron Cohen, and handsomer than Richard Burton?"
"Your first husband?"

123

"Goodnight, Harry. Joan and I had a swell time. Now I'd like to say good-bye to your wife."

"Who wouldn't?"

"Honey, why do you waste so much time washing and ironing your brassieres? There's nothing much goes in them."

"I wash and iron your shorts, don't I?"

"Darling, I think we should go out twice a week."

"Okay, you go out Tuesdays—I'll go out Thursdays."

"I just had a facial at the beauty parlor, George, how do I look?"

"Like you just blocked a drop kick."

A husband and his wife were at a tailor shop. The tailor had just measured the man's waistline. The silver-tongued little lady looked at his measurement and said:

"You know, George, it's amazing when you think of it, a Douglas fir tree with that circumference would be seventy-five feet high."

I'm not sure I like PPs (PEOPLEPUTDOWNS) when one of the communications media is used, particularly when a man puts down his own sweetie.

A man in Salt Lake City placed the following ad in the paper under *Articles for Sale:*

"Complete set of Encyclopedia Britannica. My wife knows everything."

"I just phoned the hospital to check on Mother, Willie. Good news."

"She's taken a turn for the worse?"

"You can tease all you like, Walter. I'll have you know that Mother once came in second in a beauty contest."

"Who came in first, Phyllis Diller?"

SCENE: Two couples—bridge evening.

". . . And so, soon after we were married, we were blessed with the arrival of a chubby little visitor with bow legs and no teeth."

"You had a baby?"

"No, Georgina's mother came to live with us."

END OF GAME.

"Mom, this is such a big beach. I can't decide where to build my sand castle."

"Build it on your dad's belly, Son. You'll have the tallest sand castle in the country."

"Harry, I have some good news for you and some bad news. First, I have decided to run off with Harvey White."

"Isn't that interesting. Now, tell me the bad news."

"Derek, I see here in the paper the government is going to do away with seven over-age destroyers."

"I'm sorry to hear that, darling. I'm sure you'll miss your mother very much."

"Your mother called while you were out, Margie."

"Oh, how is she?"

"Fair to meddling."

"Mother went to the beauty parlor."

"What is she having this time? Are they going to bronze her warts?"

125

"Bill, guess what, there's a new home-freezer arriving here tomorrow."

"Your mother's coming to visit?"

"Mother has decided to become a hippie, Leonard."

"This I gotta see. A size forty-six in leotards."

"Darling . . . take me to the movies?"

"I've already taken you to the movies!"

"Yes, I know you have, sweetheart. But they have 'talkies' now!"

"Darling, I know I have but a few hours to live. . . . Before I go, there's something you must know. You know we have eleven children . . . all with black hair, except one. Susan . . . she's blonde?"

"You mean Susan isn't my child?"

"No. . . no . . . Susan is YOURS; the others aren't!"

"Hello, dear. . . . This is George. I'm still down at the office. What's for supper? The same old garbage?"

"No," she answered slowly. "Actually we're having many, many things for supper."

"Yeah, what?"

"BEANS!"

"Hello, dear, this is Harry. I'm going to be late again! Working at the office."

"That's okay, dear, take your time, I'm going out anyway to buy some fire insurance on you."

"You mean life insurance, dear."

"No, I mean FIRE insurance. You're gonna be cremated when you get home."

"Darling . . . have you been cheating on me?"

"Who else?"

"Hey, honey . . . I just bought four new tires . . . what a bargain!"

"What a dummy you are! Trust you to buy tires when you don't even own a car."

"Yeah? . . . do I make comments when you buy a bra?"

"Hey, Harry! I just figured it out. You're the only guy on our block who hasn't got his own business."

"Hey, Mom and Dad, guess what? I joined the school drama club and I got my first part. I play the role of a married man."

"That's great, Son," said Dad. "Just keep plugging, one of these days you may get a speaking part."

"Gee, you're dumb, Mom. You don't know anything."

"Now, Son," scolded father, "you mustn't be picky about your mother's little faults."

"Hey, dummy, close the window, it's cold outside."
(Closing window.) "There! Now it's warm outside."

"What's Cary Grant got that I ain't got?"
"You want it alphabetically?"

"Sweetheart, you're an Amazon!"
"You mean beautiful, statuesque like those Amazon women?"
"No. I mean wide at the mouth like that Amazon river."

Man, abandoning wife at door of movie theater:
"There y'are, honey . . . I said I'd take you to the movies. Have fun, I'll be around to pick you up at ten."

Peter and Etta Fowler were on their way home from a banquet at which Peter had been the guest speaker. Etta broke the silence of the night with:

"Darling, did anyone ever tell you you were the world's best speaker?"

"No, no one ever did."

"Well, then, where did you get the idea?"

"You know, darling," he enthused, "there are two men in this world I really admire."

"Yes? . . . And who is the other one?"

"So, you're home from work. Well, that cake you asked me to bake for you . . . the dog ate it."

"That's okay, dear, don't cry . . . I'll get you another dog."

"Why do you drink so much wine, liquor, and beer?"

"Because I don't like Javex, paint-remover, or witch hazel."

"Well, at least I'm trying."

"Yes, very."

"I'd like you to meet my wife, sir."

"I hear she's a very outspoken woman."

"Yes? By whom?"

"How do you do, Mrs. Martz, I'm your husband's confidential secretary."

"Yes? . . . how nice. My husband has told me so little about you."

"I'd like you to meet my future ex-husband."

He ran into his former wife at a holiday resort and suggested to her they might . . . ah . . . go to her cabin and . . . ah . . . do the thing.

"Over my dead body," she snapped.

"Well," he shrugged. "I see nothing's changed."

"Darling, look who came to visit," purred his wife. "It's the young lady who moved in across the street last week . . . or don't you recognize her without your binoculars?"

"Hey, dummy! When the hell are ya gonna get some drapes for the windows? Do you realize if I ran through the house stark naked . . . the neighbors could see me?"

"Don't worry . . . if the neighbors see you stark naked, they'll draw THEIR drapes."

"Daddy, Mummy said I should ask you. I saw some pictures of people in my geography picture book, and they were wearing rings through their noses. What are people who wear rings through their noses called, Daddy?"

"They're called husbands, darling, they're called husbands," he repeated loudly enough for the little lady in the kitchen to hear.

"Will my smoking this cigar bother you?"

"Not if my getting sick won't bother you."

"Look, darling, let's not argue anymore. You're such a wonderful husband, I don't want to fight with you. You're such a sweet guy, that Peter O'Toole, that beautiful gorgeous man, could come up to me right now and ask me to run away with him . . . and I wouldn't forget you."

"You wouldn't?"

"Nope . . . I'd write you every day."

"Why can't you be more like Sinatra?"

"Sinatra? What's so special? Guys like him are a dime a dozen."

"Really. Here's a nickel, get me six."

George, answering telephone: "I'm sorry, Mrs. Hartley, the wife isn't in right now. Would you like to leave a rumor?"

"All I do is wait on you hand and foot . . . I'm getting fed up with it."

He remained silent.

"Did you hear what I said? I'm sick of being your slave."

He continued reading the paper.

"It might be a good idea if we wives went on strike. What do you think of that? How would you like it if I went on strike?"

"You go right ahead, dear," he said, without looking up. "I have a honey of a strike-breaker in mind."

George is greeted at the door by his wife who says:

"Hey! . . . Guess what I saw on the late, late show tonight. It was a movie from way back. Many years old. . . goes all the way back to the time you used to take me out."

"Hey, hon? Here's a job your mother should apply for."

"You're going to say something mean about my mother again, aren't you?"

"No . . . it's just that she's been looking for a job and I see here in the paper the U.S. army is advertising for someone to go to Viet Nam."

"What for?"

"To teach the marines how to fight dirty," said our hero, ducking a flying saucer.

George and Muriel had had a very large misunderstanding. Well, it was more like an argument. It was a drag-'em-out battle, is what it was.

He lost. He *always* lost.

He laid his plans carefully.

That night, they were at a cocktail party. He suddenly whipped out a large photograph of a man and began wailing,

"Oh, why did you die? . . . Why did you have to die?"

The party ground to a halt. The music stopped . . . the room fell quiet. All eyes were on the sobbing George. It was a tense moment. One man went over to comfort poor George. Placing an arm over George, he soothed:

"There, there, George, don't take it so hard. Who is this man in the picture? Was he your beloved brother?"

"No . . . this is a picture of my wife's first husband," cried George.

A husband, bored with interminable nights at home with his mate, is asked by her:

"Wouldn't it be nice if some friends dropped in?"

"Even some enemies would be welcome."

About a half-hour after a pretty good brawl with his spouse, he had cooled off a bit and tried to patch it up with:

"I'm going out to the shopping center for a few minutes, darling. What little gift can I buy for the one I love best?"

"How about a pipe and a pound of tobacco?" she shot back.

Would you believe putting down a fellow human being while he is on his death bed breathing his last? Well, it's happened, according to one story we found a few years ago. Try this one and hate the man:

The husband was standing vigil beside the bed of his

131

wife about to draw her last breath. She beckoned him to come near so she could speak. Her eyes welled up with tears as she looked at him.

"John? I know that I have little time left. I want you to promise me one thing. When I die and if you should remarry, please, John—please, don't let your second wife wear any of my clothes. Do you promise, John?"

"Sure, honey," he answered. "Besides, your stuff wouldn't fit Marjorie anyhow."

How about the poor guy who receives, on his twenty-fifth anniversary, a gift from his wife. It is a large book titled: *What I Have Learned About Lovemaking in Twenty-five Years*.

Upon inspecting the book more closely, he noted that he was listed as the author. His wife had apparently had the book specially bound and printed.

Inside? 540 blank pages.

The gentleman had a falling out with his nagging wife. She had been at him all morning. He left the house to go to work, slamming the door on the way out. Later, he phoned home.

"Sarah, what are you making for dinner?"

"What am I making for dinner? I'm making poison for dinner . . . you bum."

"Okay," he sang. "So make only one portion. I'm not coming home."

A husband and wife were on their way to a cocktail bash at the home of one of her friends. During the entire trip in the car, he gave her a pretty hard time about a lot of things, mainly about not wanting to become involved with her friends and how he didn't want to go to the damn party in the first place. By the time they arrived at the party, she was furious.

She introduced him to the hostess of the party this way:

"Beverley, remember I told you I had a drinking problem? Well, I'd like you to meet him."

Psychiatrist to patient: "The trouble with you, George, is that you are allowing your wife to dominate you completely. You go home and let her know every chance you get, that from now on you're the boss and that you're not going to allow her to push you around anymore."

George rushed home, slammed the door, grabbed his wife, and snarled:

"Look, baby, from now on, *I'm* the boss, see. This is it. When I say jump, you jump. Tonight, I'm goin' out on the town. You're gonna cook my favorite supper and then you're gonna lay out my clothes. Got it? And then, after supper, who do you think is going to dress me in my tuxedo and black tie?"

"The undertaker," answered his wife.

When a man gets put down on his wedding night, that's bad. When the squash comes from his little bride, that's cause for homicide.

As the groom gently lay beside his bride in the honeymoon suite, he suddenly turned to her and said:

"Darling, there is something I must know. Am I the first man to sleep with you?"

She looked at him tenderly, patted his cheek, and said:

"You will be, darling, if you doze off."

"...Youth is a wonderful thing. What a crime to waste it on children...."
　　　—GEORGE BERNARD SHAW

"Uncle Horace, we have a new baby at our house."

"That's nice, Billy. Did the stork bring the baby?"

"Don't be silly, he developed from a unicellular amoeba."

Mrs. Foy was showing off the knowledge of her little Ricky to a couple of neighbors who were in for tea.

"Ricky, tell Mrs. Hartman and Mrs. Waxler what the definition of heat is."

"Heat is the kinetic energy of the movement of the molecules."

"Very good. Now tell us . . . uh, let's see. What does it mean when the steam comes out of that kettle there?"

"It means you're going to open one of Dad's letters before he gets home."

"C'mon, little fella, don't cry. I know how it is."

"Yeah? How the hell is it?"

"You're not a very smart little boy. You can't even tell me how to get to John Street. Not very bright, are you?"

"Maybe not, but I ain't lost."

"You realize, son, when Lincoln was your age, he was already studying hard to become a lawyer."

"Right, Pop, and when he was your age, he was President of the United States."

A note pinned to mom's bedroom door: BE KIND TO YOUR CHILDREN AND THEY WILL BE GOOD TO YOU. SIGNED, GOD.

It was Father's Day and teacher had assigned the youngsters a composition to write entitled: "My Father."

One eight-year-old brought this one home to dad:

"My father is great. He can swim big wide rivers, climb very high mountains. He can fight tigers and jungle animals and can even beat monsters. He can wrestle alligators and jump very high. But most of the time he just takes out the garbage."

It's more than just a flesh wound when a seven-year-old puts you in your place.

A woman was taken aback when she noticed, sitting on the curb, a little boy happily puffing away on a cigarette. She walked up to him and said:

"You dirty little imp . . . does your mother know you smoke?"

The kid looked up at her and said: "Lady, does your mother know you talk to strange men in the street?"

A five-year-old watches mother apply a pound of cold cream to her face and neck. After she removes it, he observes: "Didn't work, huh?"

"Now, Jimmy, before grandma tucks you away to dreamland for the night, she's going to tell you a nursery rhyme. Ready?

"Fuzzy Wuzzy was a bear, Fuzzy Wuzzy had no hair, Fuzzy Wuzzy wasn't very fuzzy, was he? . . . Was he? . . . Well, was he?"

"Grandma, you're drunk!"

"Our Father, who art in heaven. . . ."

"I can't hear you, Johnny."

"I wasn't talking to you."

"Dad, here's my report card and a photostat of one of yours when you were a kid."

Joanie's mother was away. Dad was tucking the six-year-old into bed.

"Dad, will you kiss me goodnight like you kiss Mom goodnight?"

He gave her a kiss.

"Dad, will you lie down beside me the way you lie down beside Mom?"

He did.

"Dad, will you whisper in my ear the way you whisper in Mom's ear at night?"

He whispered in her ear.

The little girl looked at him, grabbed the blanket, turned her face to the wall, and said: "Not tonight, Howard, I'm too tired."

". . . And what will you do, Sonny, when you get as big as your Uncle Charlie?"

"Diet."

Doting aunt to bored five-year-old: "When I last saw you, you were only *so* high."

"And when I last saw you," answered the kid, "you were only *SO* wide."

"Johnny, eat your peas. Millions of kids in China would love to have those peas."

"Yeah? . . . Name two."

"Jimmy, your table manners are awful. You're a little pig. Do you know what a pig is?"

"Yeah, Pop, a pig is a hog's little boy."

"Pamela, behave! Every time you're naughty, I get another gray hair."

"Boy, Mama, you must've been a rotten kid when you were small. Look at Granny's hair."

"Pop, Billy said his pop could whip you."

"What did you say, son?"

"I said, big deal, so can my mom."

"I'm homesick."

"But you're at home, son."

"I know. I'm sick of it."

The teacher had tried every way to deal with her students. Nothing worked. . . . It seems all she got were answers that usually left her sputtering with rage. Today was no exception.

"If you were walking down a country road and in the ditch you found a man in dirty, ragged clothes, unconscious, and covered with blood from a beating he had received, what would you do? Harry?"

"I would sit down and put my head between my knees. That would keep me from fainting."

She tried another student. "What would you do, Jimmy?"

"I think I would throw up."

"Here, young man, you can't sleep in my class!"

"I could if you didn't talk so loud."

"Hey, Margie, how come you're not wearing my fraternity pin anymore?"

"Wally complains it scratches his hands."

"May I have the next dance, Judy?"

"Sure, I don't want it."

The wipeout hurts more when you're in your more tender, sensitive years.

As a teen-ager, one summer at Ile Perrot, Quebec, I was driving a lovely around the dark wood-shrouded roads looking for a place to engage in a little fancy parking. I was just slowing down when she leaned over close and whispered:

"Can you drive with one hand?"

"Yes . . . yes I can."

"Well, wipe your nose . . . it's running!"

That hurt.

In the Village, graffiti scrawled on a fence demanded: "Why are they against us taking LSD trips?"

Underneath, one of the "over-thirty" group added the line:

WE'RE NOT AGAINST YOU TAKING TRIPS—
WE'RE AGAINST YOU COMING BACK!

Teeny-bopper whispers to dancing partner:

"You know, you'd be a great dancer except for a coupla things."

"A couple of things?"

"Yeah, your feet!"

A young lovely has been sitting on the front porch with her date for three hours. He hasn't even so much as tried to hold her hand. He's just sat there like a boil all evening.

"Is there anything I can get you, Gerard?" she asked sweetly. "A cup of coffee, a Coke, a sandwich . . . 100 cc's of adrenalin?"

The science teacher thought a certain experiment would emphasize to his students the harmful effects of alcohol. During a lab period he took a dew worm, placed it in a beaker of water. The worm happily zipped around the bottom of the beaker and seemingly suffered no harmful effects from its dip. The teacher then took the same worm and placed it in a beaker of alcohol. It immediately writhed around, doubled over, and died.

"Now," said the teacher, "you all saw what happened. He survived and even seemed to enjoy the water. When I placed him in the alcohol, he died immediately. Henry Brown, what conclusion do you draw from this experiment?"

Henry's answer: "Well, sir, it's quite obvious. Drink alcohol and you'll never have worms."

The same teacher once pronounced: ". . . And so we take the example of the busy ant. He works very hard all day, takes no breaks, and is very industrious. Then what happens?"

Student: "Somebody steps on him."

"I'm looking for a beautiful gal."

"Here I am."

"Good, you can help me look."

"You know, sweetheart," he said, "since I met you, I can't eat, I can't sleep, I can't drink...."

"Why not?"

"I'm broke."

Shy boy to his first date: "Darling, I could sit here like this and look at you forever."

"Yes," she blurted, "I'm sure you could ... goodnight now."

Teen-age boy to barber: "Are you the barber that cut my hair the last time I was in here?"

"I don't know, son," sighed the barber. "I've only been here a year."

"Well, let me put it this way, Reggie. If our love affair were on TV, I'd switch channels."

Guy and girl struggling in car for about an hour. Finally she yells at him:

"Hey! ... Remember my innocence!"

He says: "Yeah ... remember?"

The teen-lad in his dad's slick convertible turned to his date as the car glided silently to the side of the road one dark night:

"Out of gas, honey," he smirked.

"Yes, I thought you might be," said his deadly date. Knowingly she produced a hip flask.

"Wow, you are a swinger, pussycat. What've you got in there—scotch or rye?"

"Gasoline!" she said, handing him the flask.

"Hey, do you know what virgins have for breakfast, Julie?"

"No, what?"

142

"I didn't think you did."

Once in a while, not often, it's the teen-ager who gets squelched. There is the old story about the biology professor who directed the following question to a lovely coed:

"What part of the human anatomy enlarges to about ten times its normal measurement during periods of emotion and excitement?"

She became very flustered and embarrassed and looking over at her fellow students, she stammered . . . .

"I . . . I don't want to answer the question."

"Very well, Miss Rogers, you needn't answer the question. Mr. Michalski, would you tell us about the part of the human anatomy we're concerned with here?"

"Yes, sir. It is the pupil of the eye that enlarges to ten times its normal size during periods of great emotion and excitement."

"Thank you, Mr. Michalski, that's quite correct," said the professor.

He turned to the young coed and said: "Miss Rogers, two things are self-evident. First, you didn't study last night's assignment, and second, I'm afraid marriage is going to be a fantastic disappointment to you."

"It's very easy for you to get straight A's in French. You were born and brought up in Paris. So quit bragging."

"Well, if that's the way it works, then you should get straight A's in geometry."

"Why do you say that?"

"Because, stupid, you're a square and you talk in circles."

This little scene opens on the front steps. A young girl has just been to a dance and has been taken to her door for goodnights. All he wants is one little kiss.

"I'm sorry, I never kiss on a first date."

"Well, okay. How about on your last?"

The young couple had been at the teen-age prom and were now sitting on her front porch. Not a word or move had emanated from the young man in about forty minutes or so. Suddenly she turned to him and said:

"George, if you had money, what would you do?"

"I dunno, I guess I'd travel," was the reply.

She looked at him tenderly, her little hand slipped into his, she pecked him on the cheek, and went inside. When he opened his hand, he found in it . . . a dime.

At the University of Toronto, a sign was once placed above a row of hooks in a cloak-room reading: FOR FACULTY MEMBERS ONLY!

Underneath, someone had graffitied: MAY ALSO BE USED FOR HATS AND COATS.

Some teen-agers, according to Soupy Sales, plan their wipeouts carefully. He tells the story about the fellow who, about to enter a phone booth, is shouldered out of the way by a teen-age girl who leaps into the phone booth before him.

"Sorry, mister," she explained. "I won't be a minute, just long enough to hang up on him!"

The school's most unpopular teacher screamed at his class:

"I want all the morons in this room to stand up!"

There was a long pause. Finally, a lone student struggled slowly to his feet.

"You consider yourself to be a moron, Sheldon?" barked the teacher.

"No, sir," offered Sheldon. "It's just that I hated to see you standing there all by yourself, sir!"

"... Some rise by sin, and some by virtue fall."
—SHAKESPEARE

"Hello, City Hall? This is Reverend Walter Donnegan calling. There is a dead mule on the road here."

"Well," said the voice on the line, "I thought you ministers look after the dead."

"We do, young man," sliced the minister. "But first we always notify the next of kin."

With those papal encyclicals on birth control and celibacy pouring out of Vatican City, priests are loathe to attend too many functions where they'll find themselves shoulder-to-shoulder with disagreeable characters waiting to pounce with their own pet theories on these subjects.

Father Havergil Horton in Los Angeles had been trying to avoid a gabby woman intent on engaging him on these touchy matters. There was no escape.

"You wish to know how I feel about celibacy, miss?" he sighed.

"It's like this. When I go to bed at night, I'm sorry; when I get up in the morning, I'm glad! Good day."

146

Reverend Bill Davidson of Cleveland once received a letter in the mail that was unsigned and contained just the word FOOL in big bold letters. He was certain it came from a disgruntled member of the congregation who was unhappy about his too progressive sermons of late.

That Sunday in church, during the announcements period, Reverend Davidson told the congregation about the anonymous letter, and added:

"I have heard of thousands of instances where a man writes a letter and doesn't sign his name to it. But, this is the first time I have heard of a man signing his name and forgetting to write the letter."

Wipe out the Pope? Impossible, you say?

Here's an ad that appeared in the Help Wanted columns of the *Montreal Gazette* the morning after Pope Paul VI published his unpopular encyclical on birth control:

> Administrative post. Retired gentleman over 65, preferably of Italian origin, wanted for executive position, large well-established religious organization. Duties to direct all activities. No previous experience in similar job necessary, though must be single. Location: central European capital. Salary to be discussed, but numerous fringe benefits. Preference given to applicant with previous record of infallibility. Apply in confidence: A.D.M. 20,000 Sherbrooke St. West, Montreal.

It is customary at most churches for the minister or priest to be at the front door of the church after the service to shake hands and have a brief word with members of the congregation as they leave the church.

One five-year-old, on the way out with his parents, asked the minister:

"How come you know so much about Hell?"

A visiting minister had been invited to conduct the service and preach the sermon at the small Southern Baptist Church in Mississippi. After the sermon, the hat was passed to help defray the traveling expenses of the visiting preacher.

It came back empty, save for three pennies.

The minister took the hat, fell to his knees, raised his eyes to heaven, and intoned:

"Dear God, I am truly thankful this day that I have been granted by thee the good fortune of getting my hat back from this congregation. Amen. And good day, brothers!"

Because clergymen teach on behalf of love and understanding and against hate and revenge and are ruled by "turn the other cheek," "love thy neighbor," and "use not the name of the Lord Thy God in vain," it becomes difficult, almost impossible, for a clergyman to put down his fellow man. . . . In fact, his job is to lift him, not destroy him.

Sometimes, however, even a priest or a rabbi is moved to do it. He must, however, to maintain the dignity of the cloth, choose his words *very* carefully.

Reverend MacNamara's Volkswagen came into collision with a twenty-five-ton truck transport. It wasn't a serious accident, but the tiny car had put the huge vehicle into a jackknife position. It would likely require hours of precise juggling to extricate it.

It wasn't really the preacher's fault, but the truck driver was furious. He came storming over to MacNamara and screamed:

"You fool, you blithering idiot—you ass . . . look at what you've done to me. Why, if you weren't wearing that collar, I'd punch you right out!"

"Young man," said the minister. "Because of my delicate station in life, obviously I can't reciprocate your abuse with that kind of language or with violence. However, let me say this. When you get home tonight, I hope your mother runs out from under the porch and bites you where you sit down!"

Here's an oldie. Since it's considered a classic, it should be included for posterity.

The Catholic priest, let's call him the Reverend Keith Randall, and Rabbi Herscovitz find themselves seated together on a flight out of Toronto. They have known each other for years and feel no discomfort at discussing subjects generally considered "taboo."

"Tell me," whispers the priest to the rabbi, "have you ever in your life had pork? Come on, Rabbi . . . you can tell me. We're old friends."

"Well . . . to be truthful, yes, I have had pork. My curiosity once got the best of me, I weakened and had a cold pork sandwich a few years ago."

"And, did you like it?" asks the priest.

"Yes, it was very pleasant . . . I enjoyed it very much. . . . Now listen to me, Father Randall. I've been honest with you. Tell me this: have you ever been intimate with a woman? Be honest now."

"Well, okay, Rabbi. If this is true-confession time, I'll tell you the truth. Yes, once, before I became ordained, I did have . . . ah . . . you know."

"Sure beats pork sandwiches, doesn't it!" squelched the rabbi.

Has God ever put anyone down? Yup.

Reverend Paul Auckland had given up for Lent the thing he loved most . . . golf. He still, however, carried his golf bag and clubs and cart in the trunk of his car.

He was driving by his favorite course and found the

temptation too much. Before he knew it, his car had turned into the golf club driveway and there he was.

"Well, I'll just drive a few off the tee, that's not really playing golf, is it?" he convinced himself. But the club felt good in his hands and the drives were all straight and true and, before he realized what was happening, he was out on the course heading for the fifth hole. An angel, who happened to be patroling in that area, spotted what was happening and immediately finked to God on poor Reverend Auckland.

"Disgusting, isn't it, boss?" said the angel. "He must be punished very severely. Why don't I let fly with a bolt of lightning, or I could have a tree fall on him, or. . . ."

"Yes, you're right, this is terrible and he must be punished, but I have a better idea. Watch him play this next hole. I've arranged a little something."

The minister teed up on a 580-foot hole, let fly with a terrific drive that sailed out about 300 yards, hit a rock and took another 100-yard bounce, hit a tree and rebounded straight up the dog's-leg right onto the green, and gently rolled into the cup.

"Hey, God! What kind of punishment is that? A 580-foot hole-in-one?"

"That's his punishment," said the Lord. "The greatest golf shot in history . . . and he can't tell anybody about it."

The country minister was preaching to the unusually crowded church.

"I'm very pleased to see such a large number of you at our Easter services. Since many of you will not be here again until next year at Easter, I'd like to take this occasion to wish you a Merry Christmas."

Here's a true story:
Radio Station CHTK, in Prince Rupert, Canada, runs one of those religious open-line programs on which lis-

teners are urged to telephone and air their most outspoken opinions on the most sacred topics.

One Sunday, last year, the subject was "God Is Dead" and the arguments raged heatedly for an hour. Then a bolt of lightning hit the transmitter and knocked the station off the air for twelve hours.

Is nothing sacred? The church bulletin on the front lawn announced in big bold type:

IF TIRED OF SIN—COME IN.

Underneath, someone had handwritten in equally bold letters:

IF NOT, CALL HICKORY 4-6798.

At the inter-church conference, a bitter verbal battle flared between a Catholic Cardinal and an Angelican Archbishop. Angry words were hurled back and forth between the two throughout the afternoon's debate. It was late when the conference finished, and the two clergymen found themselves in the uncomfortable position of having to share a taxi.

"Ah, well," conceded the archbishop. "Let us not carry our differences outside the conference room. After all, we are men of God and we both serve the same God."

"You're quite right," agreed the Cardinal. "After all, we do serve the same God, you in your way and me in His."

The *Omaha World Herald* reports the story about the clergyman who was in the habit of going up to his little girl's bedside each evening and telling her a story before she went to sleep.

One evening he told her such a thrilling tale that the youngster sat up in bed, looked intently at her father, and asked:

"Daddy, is that a true story or are you preaching?"

"You're a minister, huh?"

"Yes, I am."

"What church?"

"Baptist."

"Oh, you're the narrow-minded bunch that believes only their group is going to make it to heaven."

"I'm even more narrow-minded than that . . . I don't think all of *our* group is going to make it."

The saying is that "heaven will protect the working girl, but who will protect the guy she is working for"?

"Miss Hatfield, I was just reading over this letter you did. Your typing is really improving. I see there are only seven mistakes here."

"Thank you, sir."

"Now, let's take a look at the second line."

"Gee, Mr. Bangelstein. I hope you never get one of these. It says here in the paper that a new office machine is on the market that will replace three women."

"You mean it will go to the washroom 18 times, make 107 personal phone calls, take 5 coffee breaks, take up office collections twice a week, and get pregnant in the busy season?"

Her boss was a little Hitler. He had been making unreasonable demands on her all morning. He found fault with everything. She decided she was going to quit next payday.

That afternoon, Adolph was in conference with a very important client and was working hard trying to impress him. During their meeting he excused himself, turned on the intercom, and barked:

"Miss Harris, get me my broker on the phone immediately!"

Back came Miss Harris' voice sweetly on the intercom: "You want your broker on the line, sir? Stock or pawn?"

It was her third day at the Acme Industrial accounts office. She was beautiful, a snob, and ignored the other less-endowed girls in the office. The big boss, I don't mean the office manager, I mean MR. BIG, summoned her to HIS office just off the steno pool. Hardly anybody ever went in there except his private assistant and aides. She smiled a little smile, applied some makeup, fixed her hair, and confidently strode into HIS office making sure that the other girls could see.

"Come in, Miss Barron . . . and leave the office door open! Sit down please." He gestured.

"Miss Barron," he said, in a voice loud enough for all in the office to hear. "I am told by my aides that you are the best-looking girl we have ever had working in this office."

She smiled her appreciation.

"You dress well," he continued. "You have a nice way of making an impression on visitors and your deportment is of the highest."

"Oh thank you, sir," she gushed. "Your compliments are very pleasing."

"Enjoy them, my dear," he growled, "because now we are going to discuss your spelling and punctuation and typing!"

. . . It was a long, long walk back to that desk of hers.

Boss, dictating letter to secretary: ". . . and in conclusion, let me thank you again for the excellent work your company has done for us in the past. I'm certain our current project will conclude successfully on schedule.

"Yours sincerely, Barnaby J. Lind.

"P.S. Please excuse the spelling and the typing."

Another story concerning a secretary who had a tyrant for a boss.

In the middle of dictation, she questioned something he had said with: "But Mr. Wiley, I thought. . . ."

"Don't THINK!" he sputtered. "That's not what I pay you for. You just do as you're told and take down what I dictate and then type the letter. Now, Miss Walters, do you understand that? Take down what I say and type the letters and don't think. Now, on that basis do you wish to continue your employment here or shall I look for a young lady who can do as she's told?"

She agreed to do exactly as she was told. He then dictated a letter to a very important client, a Mr. Hertforde. Some days later, this is the letter Mr. Hertforde received:

Dear Mr. Hertforde:—The idiot spells it with an "E" . . . thinks it's aristocratic. His old man was a plumber.— with regard to your letter of—look it up—anybody who can read that handwriting deserves a medal—you ask the cost of—no scratch that—you requested an estimate on the cost of replacing the components on our model cv 176—Hey, Harry! What was your department's estimate on the Hertforde job? Two thousand?—right—Our engineers advise me that three thousand is our rock-bottom price—the extra thousand is for the damn "E" he sticks on the end of his name—Hoping to receive your esteemed order . . . and so on and so on . . . you know. . . .

Next day, Miss Walters got him to sign it without reading it, mailed it, handed in her resignation . . . and lived happily . . . ever . . . after. . . .

"When men will not be reasoned out of vanity, they must be ridiculed out of it."

—L'ESTRANGE

A Texan on holiday in Israel is being shown around the farm of an Israeli.

"My land extends from those bushes there, over to this fence, and back around to that stump over there," explained the Israeli farmer.

"Well," bragged the Texan. "Back home, I have a piece of land that's quite something. I get into my car in the morning, drive all day, and by nightfall I still haven't reached the far end of my land holdings."

"I know how it is," said the Israeli. "I once had a car like that myself."

A large group of men had collected in one corner of a New York bar. A small man was amusing the group with his uncanny skill in identifying each man's nationality by the shape of his head.

"That's a lotta bull," roared a Texan in the group. "I think you're a damn fake."

"My dear sir," said the little man, "not only can I tell a man's national origin, but I can even tell what school he attended."

"What a buncha crap," sneered the Texan. "Lemme see ya do it."

"Very well," offered the man. "Now this gentleman here, he's from Princeton. Am I right, sir?"

"Why, that's right," the fellow confirmed.

"I could tell by the cut of your clothes. Now, this man over here, he's from Yale. Am I right, sir?"

"Yes."

"I was able to tell by his manner of speech. Now, this man here, he's from the University of Toronto. I can tell by the crest on his blazer."

Then, turning to the Texan, he said in a very loud voice: "Texas A and M. Am I right?"

"Well, I'll be a. . . . How could you tell?"

"I noticed the insignia on your class ring a few moments ago when you reached up to pick your nose."

A Texas oilman on holiday became enraged when the telephone operator told him to deposit a dollar twenty-five for a long-distance call.

"A dollar twenty-five?" he yelled. "Why back in Dallas, Texas, I could call Hell and back for about a half-dollar!"

"That's true, sir. But remember, in Texas, that's a local call!"

A tourist had stopped his car by the side of the road near a Texas town to watch workmen who were digging an immense ditch.

"What's the hole for, fellas?" he asked.

"Wal," drawled one of the Texans, "that's kind of a stoopid question. But if y'all don't know, ah'll tell yuh. Every once in awhile we dig a big hole like this and bury all the SOBs around here in it."

"My, my," said the tourist. "Isn't that interesting. And tell me, when you've put all the SOBs in these parts into that there hole, who's going to be around to cover it up?"

Danny Thomas tells about the big competition that still rages between Texas and Alaska for "bigness honors in the U.S.A." For example, says Danny, there was the time a seven-foot Texan on holiday in Alaska walked into the only department store in Nome and asked for a winter sports coat for himself.

"Yes, sir," said the clerk. "Boy's wear, second floor."

For eight hours, one hot afternoon in New York, a native was showing a Texas cousin through town. The Texan was not impressed.

When the New Yorker pointed out a landmark or place of interest, the Texan invariably mentioned something bigger and better "back home."

The New Yorker bit his lip and said nothing as each new squash was administered by big-mouth, but his blood pressure was building and his adrenalin gushing with each new wipeout.

At the end of the day, as the tour was finishing, they were driving by the United Nations Building.

"There!" The New Yorker pointed to the UN Building with pride. "Isn't that a magnificent structure?"

"Well, ah guess it's okay, pal. Back home, though, we have an out-house larger than that."

"Yes, and I guess you need it!" said the New Yorker . . . and so saying, he parked the car at the curb, got out and took the subway home.

A Rhode Islander was the guest of honor at a banquet in Houston. During the cocktail hour before dinner, he got kidded about the size of his tiny state compared to Texas. He suffered the usual crowing about the great State of Texas. Even the president of the club, who introduced him at the head table, made reference to the size of his home state.

160

He got to his feet, thanked the members for their hospitality, and told the following story:

A Dallas oilman died and went to that great eternal resting place. Upon arrival there, he was surprised at the amazing similarity of the terrain to home.

"My goodness," he said to the first person he met. "I never expected heaven to be so much like Texas."

"My friend," the man said. "I'm sorry to inform you, this isn't heaven."

"The flay's the thing. . . ."

Two hard-rocks, obviously prowling for trouble, walk into Harry's Bar and Grill. One orders a scotch on the rocks and the other says:

"Bring me a rye and water and be damn sure it's in a clean glass!"

A short time later, the bartender returns and asks:

"Sorry, fellas, I forgot. Which one of you wanted the clean glass?"

"I'll have you know I have a good head on my shoulders."

"I think you have a point there."

One sadistic doctor we heard about even squelches his frightened patients.

Just before the operation a patient will look pleadingly into the eyes of the doctor and say:

"Doctor, this is my first operation . . . !"

He answers: "You, too?"

A well-dressed man with derby and umbrella entered a London department store. Suddenly, there was music, photographers, and TV cameras. A smiling master of ceremonies appeared at his side and informed him he was the lucky one to be the one millionth customer.

"And now, will you tell us and the TV audience what you came here for today?"

"Gladly," answered the customer. "I'm on my way to the complaint department."

A fellow driving his car with the top down was wearing a bright red shirt, a polka-dot tie, a shepherd's plaid suit, and a lavender beret. A motorcycle cop stopped him and made him pull over to the side of the road.

"What's wrong, officer?" asked the lad. "I haven't violated any traffic laws."

The cop said: "No, I know you didn't. I just wanted to hear you talk."

"I got a job working for a drug store. I'm supposed to increase business."

"What do you do, stand out front and make people sick?"

"Drinking makes you beautiful, baby."
"But, I haven't been drinking."
"I know, but I have."

"Boy, you're ugly, lady!"
"And you're drunk."
"Right . . . but tomorrow you'll still be ugly."

"Lazy? He doesn't walk in his sleep. He hitchhikes."

"Do you believe in free love?"
"Have I ever sent you a bill?"

165

"Dad, what do you think I should wear with these chartreuse and orange socks?"

"Hip boots."

"What's the idea telling him I was stupid?"

"It's a secret?"

"The trouble with you English is that you think you're so bloody good, you don't mingle with the other races. . . . Look at me! I've got Hungarian, Russian, Spanish, and French in my blood."

"Yes? Really? . . . Very sporting of your mother."

The tyrannical boss of the small leather factory had suffered a temporary attack of conscience for his treatment of the officers of his company. He invited his twenty supervisors and foremen to his palatial home on the hill for cocktails and dinner. They still hated him and came hoping to see something terrible go wrong with the evening. What fun it would be to see him fall flat on his fundament!

But, alas, all was going well. The cocktails were served. They were perfect. Napoleon was being the perfect host. It was turning out to be a fine show for the boss.

They all sat down to dinner. The first courses were elegantly served, and the food was great. Then, the old man got up at the head table and announced:

"Ladies and gentlemen, as a special treat for tonight, I'm pleased to tell you that we are serving a whole roast pig. Bring it in, Martha."

Martha, the cook, brought it in or at least tried to. As she entered the huge dining room she tripped on the doorsill and the roast pig went flying off the tray onto the floor and slid slowly, sickeningly across the floor, coming to rest under a portrait of one of their host's ancestors, who glared down disapprovingly.

This was it. This is what they had all been waiting for.

Hah! He's been made the fool. I wonder who planned it? Now what is the old buzzard going to do? Boy, he must be embarrassed . . . in front of all the people he's been tormenting, too. Good . . . good.

The old man calmly waited for the noise and clatter to stop . . . looked around at his guests and said:

"Ladies and gentlemen, you must forgive this unfortunate accident . . . but these things happen, you understand."

Then, addressing himself to the cook, he said:

"Martha, I wonder if you would mind picking up the pig, taking it back to the kitchen, and bringing out the OTHER roast pig!"

Lonely Hearts Club
4210 W. 116th St.
Acme, Ohio

Mr. Harold Hopkins,
342 Hollywood Crescent,
Northway, N. H.

Dear Mr. Hopkins:

Thank you for your application for membership in the Lonely Hearts Club of America. We are returning your application and photograph herewith.

We're not that lonely.

Sincerely,
Wilma Matthews,
Pres.

"Funny, I never think of you skinheads as being bald."
"Odd, I think of *you* as being very hairy."

"See here, Jones. I'm fed up with you getting your hair cut on company time."

"It GROWS on company time."

"It doesn't all grow on company time."

"I don't get it all cut off."

In England and in some east European countries, it is customary to tip the usher in a movie theater.

The scene is a London theater. The movie is a complicated murder thriller. A family of five come in and are shown to their seats. The tipping custom is not observed.

At intermission, the usher hands each member of the family a note which reads: THE CAPTAIN OF THE SHIP KILLED THE GIRL.

The proprietor of a rather large local factory in a small town was being questioned by a woman concerning his policy of hiring only married men to work for him.

"I personally think it's a good policy, mind you," she offered. "But as a wife, I can't help wondering why you hire married men only. Is it because we women have given them strength, understanding, and ambition?"

"No, madam, it's because they're used to being pushed around, can obey orders instantly, and don't sulk when I yell at them!"

In the municipal offices there was a rule. Only university graduates could be promoted above a certain level. The last three college men to assume responsible jobs with the administration bungled their efforts badly. Their departments were a mess.

A sign finally appeared just over the toilet-paper dispenser in the city hall men's room: UNIVERSITY DIPLOMAS—TAKE ONE.

Dorothy Parker once suggested that a female acquaintance had broken her leg "sliding down a barrister."

A handsome young man, who had been around, made a play for a young lady on board a luxury liner en route to Europe. She repelled his every advance, telling him:

"I think you are a bore and have the personality of a hangnail. I would find it impossible to be in your company for more than an hour."

He persisted, however, and she warmed to him after a time. He showered her with flowers and many gifts and whispered sweet suggestions into her ear.

One day, she consented to allow him into her stateroom. The lights were dimmed, the music played, they caressed. Their bodies pressed together, there was no doubt . . . she was surrendering. She led him to her bed and disrobed. Arms outstretched, she invited his embrace.

"Madam," he said. "You once called me a bore and told me you could not bear to be in my company more than an hour. The hour is up! Goodnight!"

Joe, the sharpie salesman, was in town for just the one night. He figured he'd have to work fast. He was dancing with a girl he had just met and started in for the kill.

He held her very close and whispered: "You're very lovely . . . you set me on fire."

He gave her another squeeze and said: "You're a marvelous dancer."

He nuzzled her and whispered: "In fact you're the most exquisite dancer I've ever met."

Just moments later he started in again: "Look, honey, this is the only night I'm going to be spending in this city."

"You have only tonight in our town? Isn't that a shame. . . . Tell you what, I'll dance as fast as I can."

"I'm afraid you'll have to pay full fare for that boy, madam. He looks to be at least thirteen."

"How can he be thirteen? . . . I've only been married eleven years!"

169

"Lady . . . my job is to take fares and drive the bus . . . not to hear confessions."

"Excuse me, Mr. Schreter. Do you remember that cheese you sold me yesterday? You said it was from Switzerland. Would you mind telling me about it again? Did you say it was imported or deported?"

He made an improper suggestion. Resisting the temptation to belt him, she instead whispered in his ear:
"You know what I'd like to do to you?"
"No, what?" he asked eagerly.
"I'd like to rent you out to a nearsighted knife thrower."
THEN she belted him.

The bride was fretting during the last frantic moments of preparation.
"Mother, everything has to be perfect," she cried. "We mustn't overlook the most insignificant detail."
"Don't worry, darling," soothed mama. "He'll show up."

"I'm at my wit's end."
"Short trip."

Harold Ross, founder and editor of *The New Yorker*:
"One thing I'll say for myself, I never struck a woman but once."
Franklin P. Adams: "And even then, unfavorably, I'll bet."

The class fink had turned in a dreadful final exam paper. The professor, who had tolerated his abuse and indifference through the term, was secretly delighted. He wrote the following in the margin of the corrected theme:

170

"Your vocabulary is mean and impoverished, but quite adequate to express your thoughts."

There's a true story which concerns a good-looking gal who is an airline stewardess. Two of her passengers on a Washington-New York flight were much more interested in her than in transportation.

One man did his best to persuade her to meet him at his apartment in Manhattan. The other tried and tried to persuade her to invite him to her apartment. The two, who were not seated near each other, were at least one sheet in the wind.

The first man became desperate as the plane neared New York. He went to her, gave her a key and a slip of paper, and told her:

"Take the key. The address is on the paper. Just come when you can. I'll be waiting."

She took the key, smiled, and said she would think it over. A bit later she went to the second man, who was in his seat. Without saying a word, she gave him the key and the slip of paper.

Black comic Dick Gregory tells this one:

"I walked into this restaurant in Biloxi, sat down, and was immediately told by a white waitress:

" 'We don't serve black people in here.'

" 'That's awright, honey, I don't plan to eat any black people in here. Bring me a whole chicken.' "

"Boss, I want a raise . . . and I need your answer tomorrow."

"Okay, I'll have the answer for you tomorrow . . . and it'll be no."

Pity the poor fellow who strides confidently into the boss's office to ask for a raise. Before he can open his mouth, the boss hits him with:

"Come in, George, I've been wanting to talk to you. Your name keeps popping up in the suggestion box, and. . . ."

A well-dressed but inebriated fellow at Harry's Bar and Grill created a rude odoriferous zephyr.

A man sitting on the next stool jumped to his feet, grabbed our offending friend, and said:

"How dare you flatulate before my wife?"

"Sorry, old man," said the souse. "I didn't realize it was her turn."

"You remind me of the ocean."

"You mean I'm wild, restless, romantic?"

"No, I mean you make me sick."

If you're determined to *really* put a guy down, don't insult his wife, his integrity, or his children. Insult his hometown . . . that *really* hurts. Here are a few suggested town-flatteners:

"What a hick town. The late, late show started at 7:30."

"Plug in your electric shaver and the streetlights dim."

"When they hold a parade, there's no one left to watch it."

"They had to share their horse with the next town."

"It's such a small town everybody knows whose credit is good and whose wife isn't."

"The phone book has one yellow page."

"That's not just a sleepy town . . . it's in a coma."

172

"You go to the park, see the cannon . . . that's it."

"They have one traffic light. It changes once a week."

An intense rivalry exists between the two great Canadian cities of Montreal and Toronto. Whenever Montreal's popular radio personality, Yvan Ducharme, is invited to speak in Toronto, he tells this story:

"I was here once. I remember, it was a Sunday about twelve years ago. The Royal Canadian Air Force was holding air exercises. Five thousand paratroopers were to descend on this fine city. What a tragedy. Every parachutist was killed."

Here, Yvan would pause dramatically.

"You see, they jumped out of the planes over the city and it was a Sunday. Everyone knows very well that on a Sunday, nothing opens in Toronto."

A union official looking to organize the labor force of a small manufacturing plant asked the president of the firm:

"How many people work in this sweat shop?"

Back came the answer: "About half!"

Once upon a time there was a traveling salesman who pulled up at a country farmhouse at about dusk. The farmer's daughter came out to see what he wanted.

"Any brushes today?" he asked.

"No," she replied. "But won't you stay? Father is away for a few days and I'd love to have you spend the night."

"No, thanks," answered the salesman and drove away.

There's nothing a performer enjoys more than squelching a theatrical agent.

Charles McHenry in the *New York Daily News* tells the one about the time Johnny Tillotson, the singer, was waiting for an elevator when a guy slid up to him and said:

"I know you, you're a singer. Sing something for me."

"Sure," said Johnny. "Just as soon as I find out what you do for a living."

"I'm an agent," the man replied.

"Okay," said Johnny, "let's make a deal. I'm a singer, so I'll sing you a song. You're an agent, tell me a lie."

A sweet old couple were celebrating their fiftieth wedding anniversary. They had invited their four sons and their families over for dinner. The dinner progressed smoothly 'til the old man discovered that none of the sons, all of whom were doing well, had bothered to bring an anniversary present.

Just before Mama served the coffee, the old man dramatically rose to his feet and called for everyone's attention.

"My dear and only sons, on this occasion, your mother and I have something important to tell you. We were never married."

"Do you know what that makes us?" gasped one of the sons.

"Yes, I do," replied the old man. "And damn cheap ones at that!"

During Canada's EXPO 67, before a crowd of thousands of French-Canadians, many of them Separatists, General Charles de Gaulle shouted the Separatist slogan: "Vive Le Quebec Libre." The rebels were delighted, the rest of Canada, including most loyal French-speaking Canadians, were outraged.

Some weeks later, a Separatist group was meeting in a small hotel in Montreal. One of them excused himself from the banquet hall for a visit to the men's washroom.

Over the hot-air electric hand-dryer was a sign that read: PUSH BUTTON AND HEAR A MESSAGE FROM DE GAULLE.

174

Two businessmen had been feuding for months over the alienation of certain clients. It got worse every day. It finally reached the point where one of the men was, by the sheer thievery of the other, put out of business. The victor, jubilant, decided it was time for a long and exotic holiday. He chose to cross the Atlantic on a Russian ship; once in Russia he planned to take an extended tour of the Far East.

The big day came, he boarded the Russian ship, and away he sailed. He was one day out when he received a cable from the man he had broken.

The cable read: IF YOU CAN'T SHOOT KOSYGIN, TRY FOR BREZHNEV.

An anxious and married young swinger was out for a night on the town with a coed majoring in psychology. He finally couched her and had big plans to play a little. Instead, she tormented him for an hour or so with intimate questions about himself. He was quickly falling out of love when she finally asked:

"Do you talk to your wife when you make love?"

"Yes, I do," he said, reaching for his hat and coat. "If I'm near a telephone."

George the bartender was pretty upset. The owner of the tavern was upstairs, again, being entertained by his wife. He needed the job and couldn't really do much about it.

To get even, George was giving everyone who came in booze on the house. Word got around the neighborhood pretty quickly, and soon the joint was jumping. Fights, noise, singing. It was great!

The phone rang. It was the boss upstairs.

"What the heck are you doing down there?"

"I'm doing to you down here what you're doing to her up there."

A small aircraft, piloted by a particularly unlovable playboy type, came in for a landing at a small airport. It thumped on the runway, bounced, hit the runway again, bounced . . . and finally steeled to a trembling stop ten feet off the end of the tarmac.

Having taxied to the hangar, our boy radioed the control tower.

"Tower, this is CF 176, give me my landing time for my log please."

Back came the quiet answer:

"Tower to CF 176—repeat please."

"Are you deaf? I want my time of landing."

"Yessir . . . which one?"

Myer and Chaim were good friends. They liked each other, but there was one serious problem that existed between them. No matter what Chaim did, Myer did it better. Myer always seemed to come out on top.

One day, Chaim got a call at home. It was Myer.

"Chaim, I'm calling you from a telephone in my car. Isn't that something? Not many people have telephones in their cars, do they, Chaim?"

Chaim went straight out and had a telephone installed in his car. He was sailing along the highway and decided to call up Myer in his car.

"Hello, Myer? This is Chaim. Listen, I'm calling you from. . . ."

"I can't talk to you now, Chaim, I have a call coming in on the other line."

It's bad enough when one person puts you down, but when an entire tribe of Indians sticks it in you. . . .

Take the story of the campaigning high-pressure politician who was addressing a rather large group of Indians just a few days before election time.

176

"My friends, I shall see to it that the government helps you!"

"Ug mum waga," shouted all the Indians.

"I shall see to it that you get better housing!"

"Ug mum waga," responded the Indians.

"I shall see to it that you get relief and annual Federal grants."

"Ug mum waga."

"I'll see to it that your children have better schools!"

"Ug mum waga . . . ug mum waga . . . ug mum waga . . ." the Indians screamed.

After the speech, our friend was feeling pretty good about the response he got to his speech. He was chatting with the chief about their problems, when he suddenly noticed a splendid herd of prize bulls in the meadow not far off.

"I wonder, Chief, if I might go into that meadow to examine those magnificent animals. I've always admired good cattle."

"Certainly you may go into meadow," replied the chief. "But be careful you don't step into any of the ug mum waga."

Ever try to get a doctor to make a house call? Ever?

One fellow we know got even. He called the doctor at three in the morning.

"Hello, is this Dr. Williamson?"

"Yes, it is. What do you mean? It's three A.M.!"

"How much do you charge for a house call?"

"Twenty-five dollars."

"And how much do you charge for an office appointment?"

"Five dollars, but. . . ."

"Okay, Doc, I'll meet you in your office in half an hour."

177

"My wife doesn't understand me," wailed the drunk to his fellow bar-flies for the seventy-seventh time.

Turning to his closest neighbor again, he cried: "My wife doesn't understand me, does yours?"

"I don't know," quipped his exasperated victim. "She never mentions you."

There is a place in Spain where the law requires a man who gets a girl pregnant out of wedlock to pay a given sum of money every week for sixteen years to support the child. A certain gypsy had been faithfully making the payments for almost thirteen years. During the last two or three years, the mother had been sending the child to collect the money from her father.

One day, when the girl arrived, he smiled and said:

"You go home and tell your mama that this is the final payment, and then watch the expression on her face."

The girl did as she was told, but was back in half an hour with the following message:

"I told Mama that this was the final payment and that you said I should watch the expression on her face. Well, she said if this is the last payment, I should tell you that you're not my father . . . and I should watch the expression on YOUR face."

A lovely Indian waitress in a roadside restaurant was being annoyed by a two-bit Cassanova with come-on's like:

"Indian Princess do it for a buck?" and. . . .

"How about Indian Princess go into forest with white man?"

"Come on, honey, you wanna make whoopee with me? Tell me in Indian."

She looked at him for a long time and said: "UGH!"

178

Sometimes having the right words at your command is better than a genuine wipeout.

A young technician on duty in the master control room of a gigantic electric power complex was asked to demonstrate the operation to a group being shown through the plant. The visitors' host was no less a personage than the president of the company.

The young man deftly threw switches, pressed buttons, and turned dials. Computer tapes whirled, lights flashed, electric arcs cracked across the room, and smoke poured out of the infernal apparatus. Then all was quiet. The machine died. The engineer had wrecked the panel that controlled electric power to almost half of the U.S.A.

The company president, embarrassed and furious, sputtered: "Well? Now what are you going to do?"

"I'm going to buy a small farm in Ohio, sir."

A young thing, known to be a swinger, was approached at a cocktail party by one of the local lads with:

"Hi, kid, how about letting me take you home. I love experienced girls."

"Why you no good, rotten . . . I'll have you know I am not an experienced girl."

"You're not home yet, either."

"Honey, what would I have to give you for one kiss?"
"Chloroform."

"Man, I'm sad today," said the aging would-be lady killer. "The doctor told me last night I have to give up half my sex life."

"Which part are you going to give up?" asked one of his bored listeners. "Talking about it or thinking about it?"

Franklin P. Adams, New York columnist, once asked Algonquin Hotel Manager Frank Case about a certain unpopular playwright, generally hated by his colleagues for his cheapness.

"Haven't seen him lately," said Case. "But, I hear he went out to buy a ring for his fiancée and got his finger crushed between two pushcarts."

Dear Mr. Walter:

Thank you for your invoice for $187.00 for the shelf you built recently in my kitchen. Although I think your bill is outrageously high, I am enclosing a check in payment because I believe you are a real expert in your job. Expert: Ex, meaning has-been; and, spurt, meaning a drip under pressure. You're expert.

Yours sincerely,

Mrs. P. Lapp

The professor of English, though a loveable guy, had a reputation for using rough language and telling bawdy tales in class. Naturally, his class contained few coeds. The girls who DID attend his lectures however were subjected to his regular habit of dispensing lewd, locker-room humor.

They decided the time had come to do something. Next time the professor began his nonsense, all the girls would get up immediately, leave the classroom, and go straight to the dean's office. Good strategy. But the professor had been tipped-off and was ready for them.

Next morning, as soon as the class settled in, he held up a newspaper and announced:

"I've just been reading here in the paper where the government has decided to ship all the prostitutes to Viet Nam."

That was it! The coeds got up and started for the door.

"Oh, don't rush off now, girls. Relax. The first boat doesn't leave for a week."

He had just asked her the oldest question in the world. She replied:

"I'm afraid that my awareness of your proclivities in the esoteric aspects of human propagation precludes you from such a confrontation."

"I don't get it," he said.

"That's right," she said.

Fed-up office worker, having martinis at his desk, to boss:

"Hope you don't mind, sir. Just having a little celebration on the tenth anniversary of my last raise."

This story concerns a young sharpie who barges into the office without knocking and demands: "Say, buddy, do you have an opening for a smart young man like me?"

"Yes, we do," said the irritated personnel manager. "And please don't slam it on your way out!"

A rough type walked into a department store, purchased a large cigar, lit it, and created a huge smoke screen. The salesgirl politely informed him that smoking was not permitted in the store.

"What? That's ridiculous!" he shouted. "You sell cigars here . . . why can't I smoke?"

"That's right, sir, we *do* sell cigars and smoking *is* prohibited, but we also sell bath towels and contraceptives."

In the *Montreal Star,* Bruce Taylor reports the Rexall Drug Company wired U.S. Senator Lee Metcalf to protest the high cost of what it called the "amazing" bill to increase social security benefits below the border. Senator Metcalf shot back this telegram:

"That a DRUG company should be amazed at the price of anything amazes me."

Touché!

There were two men in a bar, a Hungarian and a Yugoslav. They were arguing about which is the better all-'round nationality. The Hungarian argued hard for his people and ran down the Yugoslavs. The other praised everything about the Yugoslavs and insulted the Hungarians.

Finally, the Yugoslav said in a loud voice for all to hear: "Okay, maybe there *is* something special about you Hungarians. I heard a story the other day that I must tell you. A cannibal walked into a cannibal restaurant, looked at the menu, and was a little puzzled. It read: Germans $4.50; Yugoslavs $5.10; Italians $3.75; Frenchmen $5.45; and Hungarians $48.50.

" 'Hey,' " said the cannibal. 'These prices are all great, waiter, except for the Hungarians. How come you're charging $5.45 for a Frenchman and you charge $48.50 for a Hungarian?'

" 'It's cheap at that price,' replied the waiter. 'You ever try to clean one of them things?' "

McKenzie Porter, *Toronto Telegram* columnist who frequently expresses his outrage at the way men's fashions are going, subscribes to the Adolphe Menjou school of impeccable dress for the man of today. Turtleneck sweaters are unthinkable. Brown shoes with black suit? . . . sir!! Narrow-brimmed hats? Never, sir! And very bad taste to wear a Tartan to which one is not entitled.

This has given Porter the disadvantage of having to hear opinions on men's fashions from would-be correct dandies. At one cocktail party, a particularly obnoxious fellow kept badgering Porter with silly questions about "correct" dress for men.

"What, for example, would you wear with a brown suit after five P.M.?" he demanded.

Porter looked at the man and said: "Bicycle clips, sir!"

The trend to long hair this decade may be the result of males all over the world deciding that barbers talk too much. Have you noticed? The minute you sit in that chair . . . the marathon begins. And, have you noticed how many of the snippers fancy themselves comedians and make unkind remarks about your receding hairline or your baldness?

It isn't often that a barber is put in his place, mainly, I suppose, because they just don't stop talking long enough to be put down.

"My goodness," said the barber running his hand over the hairless pate of a customer. "You know the top of your head feels exactly like my wife's derriere?"

Much laughter from the other waiting customers . . . after all, it *is* a cute line. Our bald friend waited for the laughter to subside, reached up, rubbed his head, turned to the barber, and in an equally loud voice declared:

"You know, it DOES feel like your wife's derriere."

Mr. Bragg, at the poker club: ". . . No, sir, you'll never catch me looking at women other than my wife. I'm too decent, too fine, too good. . . ."

"Too old," added one of the card sharks.

Sometimes you can put a man down . . . and pay the consequences, without uttering a word. Terence Duff tells this story in *Weekend* Magazine.

"A Glasgow man was fined $15.00 recently for parking his Rolls Royce on a policeman's foot.

"The constable testified that the driver became angry when told he could not leave his car at the city's rail terminal. The driver rolled the Rolls back on to the policeman's foot, locked the car, and walked off. Onlookers tried in vain to free the constable; he couldn't move until the driver returned, and his foot was badly bruised.

"The driver, who denied he deliberately drove onto the policeman's foot, was convicted of assault."

A salesman once sent a wire to his boss which read: EITHER MEET MY TERMS OR COUNT ME OUT.

Back came the reply: ONE TWO THREE FOUR FIVE SIX SEVEN EIGHT NINE TEN.

"Hey you! Are you the foreman? I hear you're planning to fire my son. I hope you haven't got anybody in mind for the vacancy!"

"Madam, your son won't leave no vacancy!"

A father was wheeling his twin babies along the walk when a woman dashed over, made a big fuss over the two babies, and finally asked the question that really deserved no reply: "My, aren't they cute . . . are they twins?"

"No, madam . . . of course they're not twins . . . I have TWO WIVES!"

A letter is usually the coward's way to the great wipeout, but often it's the most powerful. Witness the letter sent by a hostess to a couple who had attended a cocktail party at her home.

Dear Joan and Bill:

You dropped the following names at our house last night. Thinking you might need them, I am returning the lot herewith.

Be sure, when you're out on the patio with your favorite gal, that you're entertaining her. You might be the victim of a squash as big as the one poor Bill got one night.

He was at a house party, out on the patio with one of the local beauties. She turned to him and said:

"I feel a little chilly, Bill, I wonder if you would mind going back in and bringing me out John Hartman?"

The incomplete explanation is maddening. Walk up to someone and say: "The boys and I had a good laugh about you today." That's all. No more. Hurts, eh?

The late Sammy Sales, Canadian funnyman, used to tell the story about the guy in a Miami hotel who asked for a five-dollar suite.

The clerk gave him a chocolate bar!

A modestly dressed, quiet Milquetoast arrived at the front desk of a chromy, big-city hotel.

"I'd like a single room, please, for two nights."

"Are you kiddin', buster?" the too-slick clerk snarled. "We don't have any rooms at all . . . you'll have to go someplace else." And so saying, dismissed the fellow.

"Excuse me," persisted the fellow. "I really need this room."

"Look, I said there ain't any . . . now blow!"

"Excuse me, but if the President of the United States came here, you'd have a room for him, wouldn't ya?"

"Well, I guess we would if it was the President."

"Well, gimme his room . . . he ain't comin'."

A shaggy-haired sharpie in a seersucker suit, driving his dad's new convertible, pulled up beside a young thing about to board a bus. Removing a ten-cent cigar from between his teeth, he leered at her:

"I'm headin' south, honey."

She looked at him long and hard, smiled, and said, "You heading south? Really?"

185

"Yeah, honey!"

"Bring me back an orange," she said, boarding the bus.

A great many of the best wipeouts are one liners, and often they are plays on words:

"I think the stork that delivered you made a crash landing."

"Say, you've really got something there. I hope it's not catching."

"He's having business troubles . . . can't mind his own."

"He has been educated beyond his intelligence."

"He has the situation in the hollow of his head."

"You look like an unmade bed."

"She's a girl you look at twice . . . the first time you don't believe it."

"Of course I'm planning to invite you to my party, Barbara, there's always room for one bore."

"I can't decide whether she looks exotic or exhausted."

"I need her like Richard Burton needs a recreation room."

"She's worth her weight in gall."

"I always thought those alcoholics were anonymous."

"His mother should have thrown him away and kept the stork."

"She's been around more than a revolving door at Simpson's-Sears."

"She's seen more life than a policeman's flashlight."

"I've heard nicer music come out of a leaky balloon."

"I've heard pickle barrels that sloshed better than that."

"Who does your arrangements? . . . the Salvation Army?"

"He's playing under a handicap tonight . . . he's sober."

"Say, I've heard a lot about you. Now I'd like to hear your side."

"Goodnight, Mr. Hargreaves, It's been great no-ing you."

"His idea of big time is to turn up his electric blanket."

"Say, I didn't know you couldn't sing."

"And, when this crisis is all over, George, I'll always remember you as a tower of weakness."

"Hi, beautiful! Lookin' for a lift? How far ya going?"
"Not that far."

"She has gold-digger rash. An itch for a guy with scratch."

"She's not completely useless. Five charm schools are using her as a bad example."

"His get up and go, got up and went."

"One day he's gonna march into an unemployment office and surrender."

"There's only one thing wrong with you. You're visible."

A lady was suing a man for insulting her in a public place. He had apparently called her a fat horse. The judge reprimanded him and fined him fifty dollars.

"Your honor, are you telling me I can never call a lady a fat horse again?"

"That's right," said the judge.

"Well, okay. But tell me, judge, is it all right to refer to a fat horse as a lady?"

"I guess so," said the judge. "Yes, I'm sure there's no law against calling a fat horse a lady."

Whereupon, the accused turned to the woman, raised his hat, and said: "Good morning, lady."

"But why can't I marry your daughter, Mrs. Hinkle?"

"Because if you want to know the truth, I think you're effeminate."

"Gee, Mrs. Hinkle, compared to you, I guess I am."

"Whisky and sofa?"

"Nope, gin and platonic."

"Hello, Police Department? I've lost my cat and. . . ."

"Sorry, sir, that's not a job for the police, we're too busy. . . ."

"But you don't understand . . . this is a fantastically intelligent cat. He's almost human . . . he can practically talk."

"Well, you better hang up, sir. He may be trying to call you right now."

"I'm planning a salary increase for you, young man."

"When does it become effective?"

"Just as soon as you do."

In Beverly Hills, California, a wealthy film producer, who was an amateur horticulturist, tended his own shrubs and flowers for the pure love of it. He was busy pruning his favorite rose bushes along the edge of his drive, when a block-long Rolls Royce pulled up carrying a wealthy and rather unpleasant woman whose estate was a short distance away. She had been desperately trying, unsuccessfully, to engage a gardener for her grounds.

Thinking to steal one from a neighbor, she pointed her finger at our friend, and said:

"You! . . . Yes, you. How much does the lady of this house pay you to look after her garden? I'll double whatever it is. How much does she pay? Well, come, young man, I haven't all day. How much does she pay?"

"Well," said our hero. "She actually doesn't pay me anything for my services, but she does let me sleep with her once in awhile."

Careless big-mouth barber to customer: "Have I shaved you before, sir?"

"No, I got these scars in Viet Nam."

Canadian radio's DeMille, Andrew Allen, to pest at cocktail party:

"I have always hated bores, but I particularly hate boring amoebas."

It hurts bad enough when you are quietly squelched by a fellow in a private place. But it isn't cricket when you're publicly denounced by a posted sign. This one was spotted on a western Canadian farm.

ATTENTION HUNTERS. USE EXTREME CARE. DO NOT SHOOT ANYTHING THAT ISN'T MOVING. IT MAY BE MY HIRED MAN.

Rich man who had not made a contribution to the Community Chest appeal in years, received a blunt note from the annual drive committee, inquiring why he was not contributing his fair share.

He wrote back:

189

Gentlemen:

In answer to your query about my lack of support for the Community Chest, let me say this!

I have a brother, Henry, living in Watertown, N.Y. He is an alcoholic with a wife and three children.

My aging mother is an invalid incapable of working and not eligible for pension.

My father is a compulsive gambler accumulating staggering debts weekly.

My younger brother, Julian, married, with four children, just went bankrupt out east.

My four sons want to go to college.

Now, here is my point. If I'm not helping my alcoholic brother Harry, or my crippled mother, or my gambling father, or my bankrupt brother Julian, and I don't plan to send my four sons to college, why the hell would I give *you* any money?

Sincerely,
Harvey Boxwood

"Doctor, my cat hasn't been home in two nights."

"Nothing to worry about . . . it's just that she's in season. She's busy making love."

"Would she come back if I left a piece of liver on the front doorstep?"

"Would YOU?"

"I'm sorry, honey, I thought you were my mother."

"I couldn't be, I'm married."

"The President has personally asked me to help in the 'Beautify U.S.A.' project."

"Really? And which country have you decided to move to?"

Put a man down from the grave? Why not? There are at least two cases on record.

The will of a fantastically wealthy eccentric was being read to the assembled relatives.

". . . And to that good-for-nothing nephew Charlie, who I promised to remember in my will: Hi there, Charlie!"

Another will read this way:

". . . And so, being of sound mind and body, I bequeath everything to my wife, Sadie. There is one condition. She must re-marry again within a year. Then, I can be sure that there'll be at least one person who is sorry I died."

Here's a triple:

Noticing a sign outside a general store reading: WE SELL YARD GOODS, our hero walked in and asked for a yard of cider.

Unblinking, the shopowner placed the yardstick on the counter, dipped his finger in the cider, and drew a line the length of the stick.

It looked bad for our friend. Then he said:

"That's fine . . . roll it up and I'll take it home."

"Okay, buddy, move along. No loitering allowed in this town."

"Just don't you be rude, officer. I'm a Delta, you know."

"Mister," snapped the cop. "I don't care if you're a whole damn peninsula, you'll have to move along."

"Will you join me, honey?"

"You're coming apart?"

A British columnist described Beatle John Lennon's gaudy new Rolls Royce this way: "It's very much in the mood of the moment—ugly, uncharming, and a pretentious bit of anti-taste."

"You, sir, are a pain in the neck."
"Well, I have a much lower opinion of you, sir."

"You're fired!"
"Hah! . . . Fired? . . . I always thought slaves were sold!"

Dear Machine:

How are you?
This is my ninth letter to you in the past six months. Can't you get anything right? You continue to bill me for a dinner at Zelda's Bar and Grill in Budapest, Aug. 19, 1968. The closest I have ever been to Budapest is Gander, Newfoundland, in Canada.
Please correct and acknowledge. If not corrected by next month, I shall bend, tear, staple, fold, and otherwise mutilate your goddamn card!
Now get the lead out of your refractor.

Love,

Charles Brood,
Dallas, Texas

A man likes to feel his woman is his . . . and at least relatively inexperienced. The two spent bodies embraced, he kissed her tenderly, pushed her back gently, looked deeply into her eyes for a long time, and asked:
"How many were there before me?"
She looked at him in silence for a long time. Minutes passed.
"Well," he said. "I'm still waiting."
"Well," she replied. "I'm still counting."

The gentleman rarely bothered to draw the blind and was frequently seen walking around nude or with just a towel draped around his middle. Three girls sharing the apartment opposite finally left a note pinned to his door: COURSE IN ANATOMY NOT APPRECIATED.

He scribbled a note and slipped it under their door. The note read: COURSE, OPTIONAL.

"Harry, will you love me always?"

"Sure, sweetheart. Which way would you like to try first?"

A nouveau-bitch movie starlet, miffed at not being served immediately at a restaurant frequented by much brighter lights than she, complained to the waiter:

"Garçon, my friends and I have been here for ten minutes. Have you the faintest idea who I am?"

"No, m'am, I don't," came the instant reply. "But just you sit there and I'll try and find out for you."

In a small midwestern town, where the natives cherished their privacy and resented greatly the big-city types who came through their town, a motorist, stopped at the only traffic light, asked the town's lone constable:

"Hey, buddy, what's the speed limit in this here hick town?"

"There ain't any, mister," drawled the police officer. "You fellers can't get through fast enough for us."

"Honey, you look like a million bucks."

"Yes, and I'm just as hard to make."

"I just drink to quiet my nerves."

"You must have the world's noisiest nerves."

The Rod and Gun Club's champion bore, braggart, and liar was at it again:

"There I was in a clearing in the jungle," he related. "I quickly raised my rifle and fired four shots . . . and there, twenty-five yards ahead of me, lay a gigantic dead lion."

"Sounds great, George," said one of his *pals*. "Any idea how long he'd been dead?"

London, Canada's radio wizard Bill Brady tells this one.

Bill and Herman were boyhood pals. They were born and brought up in the same neighborhood, went to the same public and high schools and on to university together. They liked each other well enough, but a very keen competition was always there. They delighted in putting each other down at every opportunity . . . at any cost.

After they had both graduated from university they went their separate ways to pursue their own careers. Bill went into the army and after twenty years became a three-star general. Herman entered the clergy and after twenty years became a bishop. They had both done well.

They had not seen each other in those twenty years when, suddenly, they came face to face at a train depot. They pretended not to recognize one another.

The bishop, in his long clerical garb walked up to the general in full uniform and said: "Tell me, station master, when does the train go to London?"

"In twenty minutes," replied the general. "But, in my opinion, madam, do you really think it is wise to travel in your condition?"

". . . And so, ladies and gentlemen, time to welcome you to another edition of Mid-Morning Melodies. A half-hour radio presentation of this station. No show on this station would be complete without some Lawrence Welk records . . . so let's just consider this program incomplete, shall we?"

In this age of specialization in medicine, general practitioners understandably display some irritation when the inevitable "do you specialize, Doctor?" question is asked.

An unidentified doctor in Las Vegas hit back with:

"Madam, I *do* specialize. I specialize in the skin and its contents."

Today's farmer is no longer the bumbling overall-clad clod that the movies depicted for so many years. Perhaps he never was.

Real-estate sharpies often try to buy up prime land from farmers, thinking they're dealing with Pa Kettle or one of the Beverly Hillbillies. We heard about one slicker in Orlando who told a farmer he would like to buy about seven hundred dollars worth of his land.

"Okay by me, fella," said the farmer. "I'll sell you seven hundred dollars worth of this here land. You bring a bucket around noon tomorrow and I'll fill it up for you."

"Mister, can you help a guy out?"

"Sure, which way did you come in?"

"Mister, would you give me a quarter for a sandwich?"

"I dunno. Lemme see the sandwich."

A young man in predominantly French-speaking Quebec City in Canada was flatly turned down for a sales position that he had applied for. He demanded to know why he had been refused.

"Is it because you're prejudiced against the English-speaking Canadian?" he demanded.

"Not at all, my boy," assured the personnel officer. "Let me explain it by telling you a story:

"Once upon a time, a cat outside a mousehole tried every way to get the mouse to come out into the open. Then the pussycat got a great idea . . . she barked!

"Thinking a dog had come and chased the cat, the mouse ventured out and was immediately devoured by the cat.

"The cat, while cleaning its whiskers after a delicious repast of mouse à la carte, was heard to remark: 'It pays to be bilingual.' "

A very happy and proud fisherman was dragging a fifty-pound muskelunge fish he had caught into the trunk of his car as a kid with twelve tiny fish came by.

"Not bad, eh?" he said to the boy. "What do you think of that?"

"Caught only one, eh?"

The Canadian Broadcasting Corporation's Rex Loring tells this one. He credits the line to the late Leonard Brockington, Q. C.

The counselor, his ire erect, answered a letter this way . . . (in part).

". . . And you may place it in the hands of your solicitor or any other part of his anatomy your ingenuity may devise, or his complacency permit."

"Look, mister, leave me alone. You're old enough to be my father."

"That's entirely possible. What was your mother's name?"

"Excuse me, miss, I. . . ."

"No, I've never met you," she cut him off. "You haven't seen me in pictures or on stage. I didn't go to school with you. I know I'm good looking and I'm not shy. I don't happen to be going your way, and I wouldn't ride with you on a bet. Furthermore, I'm engaged to a 225-pound wrestler who is due here in about two minutes. Now, were you going to say something?"

"Only that you're losing your underpants."

The officer had chased and caught a convertible doing ninety. The driver snatched the speeding ticket out of the cop's hand and sneered:

"And just what am I supposed to do with this?"

"Keep it," said the policeman. "And when you've collected four of them, you get a bicycle."

"Darling, I want to get married."

"Waugh! Who'd have you?"

"Which would you rather give up," asked the matron as she snuggled up to his vest. "Wine or women?"

"That, my dear lady, depends entirely on the vintage."

I'm certain no one has ever been put down by a budgie or a parrot . . . but, broadcaster Phil McKellar insists it really happened.

A budgie named Peter, sick of the same old question: "Hello, little birdie, can you talk?" finally answered: "Yeah . . . I can talk, can you fly?"

"Oh, officer . . . can you tell me the best way to get to the General Hospital?"

"Sure, lady, just stand right where you are."

A guest conductor of a symphony orchestra was driven almost out of his mind by the fact that none of the musicians could be counted on not to skip a rehearsal. After the last rehearsal was completed he tapped the stand with his baton and announced:

"I want to take this opportunity to publicly thank the

first violinist. He is the only member of the orchestra who attended every rehearsal."

The first violinist smiled in a cordial manner and replied:

"Well, it seemed to be the least I could do since I don't plan to show up for the concert tonight."

"My dear sir, you may be interested to know that I have a B.A., a B.Sc., an M.D., and a Ph.D."

"So why don't you get a J.O.B.?"

You always feel so good and warm when a braggart and liar gets his. Especially if it is well-witnessed by his acquaintances.

Take the story of the small rancher having a talk with the boys at the local tavern:

"Well, boys, this looks like a good month for me. I'm about to ship five hundred head of bulls down to Mexico. What do you think of that?"

"I think," said one of the men at the table, "that you are a big bull shipper."

Boss, looking over shoulder of unsuspecting employee playing solitaire:

"The red six on the black seven and the pink slip in the white envelope."

A would-be novelist submitted a story titled *Why Do I Live* to a publisher. The manuscript was returned, not with the traditional rejection slip, but in an unorthodox way. The editor simply wrote in under the title *Why Do I Live?,* a line that read: "Because you MAILED it in . . . that's why."

A young man's advances had been thwarted with humiliating regularity by his sweetie. He decided to break it off, but not before he could taste the sweetness of the put-down.

He steered the conversation around to the act of sex. "I just wouldn't do it . . . that's all," she insisted. "It's something I'm saving for my husband-to-be."

"Tell me," he asked, "how would you react if a millionaire offered you one hundred thousand dollars? Would you do it then?"

"Well, I guess I would for THAT . . . I mean a hundred thousand dollars!"

"Would you for five dollars?" he pressed on.

"I would not!" she spit at him. "What do you think I am?"

"We've established that," he said, grabbing his hat. "Now we're just haggling about price!"

In New York, it's reported by a usually reliable busy-spy friend, a man boarded one of the smelly beasts there and, though there was plenty of room in the bus, he stood directly behind the driver, pestering him with small talk. The unwelcome passenger noticed one of those little novelty shrunken heads sitting in front of the driver.

"What the heck is that?" asked the bug.

"That," said the driver through clenched teeth, "is a chap who didn't move to the back of the bus when I asked him to."

Here's an oldie we're including to assure a complete record of the world's great wipeouts.

A teen-age girl arrived on the farm of an uncle and was being shown around by her teen-age cousin. They came to a pasture where the bovine species were practicing that which assures the propagation of their kind.

"Oh, look at that," said the country lad. "Would I ever like to be doing the same thing right now."

"Go ahead, pal," said the girl. "It's your cow!"

Bruce Taylor in the *Montreal Daily Star* reports one of his favorite squelches:

There's a piece in the Better Business Bureau's *Bulletin* about a fellow who ordered a gasoline engine from a mail-order house.

"Send it to me," he wrote, "and if it's any good, I'll send you my check."

Back came the answer: "Send your check. If it's any good, we'll send the engine."

Disc jockey Joe Van once got a letter from one of his listeners. It was short, and not so sweet:

Dear Joe:

I listen to your program from time to time and I want you to know that there's never a dull moment on your show. It lasts the whole program.

Toronto's "Jay" Nelson once received a letter from a female listener:

Dear Mr. Nelson:

Since you came on the air, my husband won't leave the side of the radio. He's afraid somebody'll turn it on.

CBC's Elwood Glover once received a note from a Calgary listener that read:

Dear Mr. Glover:

Since you came on the air, I find that I can still get quite a lot on my radio. I got twenty dollars on it down at the pawnshop last week.

Dear Mr. Boliska:

I heard your radio show for the first time today. Gee, I thought my razor was dull.

A suburban lady answered her front doorbell to find a little man with a black bag standing there.

"I'm the piano tuner," he announced.

"But I didn't call for a piano tuner."

"I know, one of your neighbors did."

"Darling, what happens to all the grocery money I give you every week?" asked the husband, sadly looking at the bills at the end of the month.

"Stand sideways, honey . . . and look in the mirror."

"Has anyone ever told you how wonderful you are?"

"Nope."

"Well, then, where did you get the idea?"

A politician stormed into a small midwestern newspaper and demanded to see the editor.

"Well, you finally did it, didn't you? Your hate campaign has finally worked. You've put me under so much pressure lately I've been forced to resign. The least you can do is report my resignation in your rotten rag tomorrow without any unnecessary sarcasm."

The editor promised that the resignation would be reported the following day without comment. He kept his word. The resignation was duly reported, without editorial comment, in the paper next day. It was in the column called "Public Improvements."

Don Dederal reported this one in the *Arizona Republic*.

Recently, a youth, with long, curly hair down to his shoulders, entered the Agnes Miller Boys' Club. He asked Larry Ciulla at the front desk if he could take a swim. Larry explained that for health reasons there was a rule prohibiting long-haired boys from using the pool.

"Get a hair cut," said Larry, "and you're welcome."

"Some of history's greatest men had long hair," said the young man.

Larry repeated: "Those are the rules."

The youth went on: "Moses had long hair."

Larry didn't hesitate: "Moses can't swim in our pool, either."

Mrs. Herscovitz entered Chaim's Delicatessen and asked for a smoked herring. Chaim reached down into the herring barrel and brought out a nice smoked herring, the last one in the store.

"Here look, Mrs. Herscovitz, what a fine herring this is. Shall I wrap it?"

"Well, it's nice, but I really was looking for a slightly bigger one."

Chaim, not wishing to lose the sale, put the herring back in the barrel and pulled it out again.

"Here look, this one seems just about perfect . . . shall I wrap it?"

Mrs. Herscovitz was on to him . . . she hadn't been shopping in delicatessens for thirty years for nothing.

"Tell you what," she said. "I've changed my mind. I'll take both of them."

Mr. and Mrs. Lind are out for a walk. Mr. Lind has been giving the little lady a pretty hard time. They meet her psychiatrist along the way. Here comes the wipeout.

"Why, Dr. Dorbenfeldt," she gleefully greeted him. "How nice to see you. I'd like you to meet my husband, he's one of the men I've been telling you about."

A patient wakes up in a hospital room after being in a coma for about a month.

A nurse and doctor are at his bedside and explain what it's all about.

"How do you feel?" asked the doctor.

"I feel like I want to eat something. You say I've been in a coma for a month . . . I feel like sinking my teeth into something."

"Oh, we've been feeding you all this time intravenously. There are tubes connected to your ankles and wrists. Reach down and feel," suggested the doctor.

"Look," demanded the patient. "You can have tubes from here to tomorrow, I'm hungry and I'd like something to eat. Now please bring me a hamburger or something."

"Don't be such a cry baby," admonished the doctor.

"That's right," the nurse added. "Don't be so stupid about this. It's not bad at all. The tubes will be it for awhile. Now quit your damn complaining."

"Okay . . . you're right, I guess," said the patient. "But tell me, do you have any more of those tubes around?"

"Of course we have."

"Would you bring two more in here at noon?"

"Whatever for?"

"I'd like you both to join me for lunch."

A police officer directing traffic tried to whistle down a car that ignored his hand signal to stop. He commandeered a passing car and finally, several blocks later, managed to get the offending vehicle pulled over.

"Why didn't you stop when I blew my whistle?" he demanded of the lady driver.

"Well, officer . . . I'm really quite deaf . . . and. . . ."

"That's okay, m'am . . . you'll get your hearing in the morning."

A long-standing, mainly friendly, competition exists between Canada's two largest cities, Montreal and Toronto. Toronto announcer Bob Laine came on the air one night with: "Whup . . . just a moment, folks. Somebody just handed me a letter. Hold it, it's from Montreal, I can tell it's from Montreal by the stamp. The Queen is holding her nose."

A state trooper stopped a vehicle on the turnpike for going too fast. He walked up to the driver behind the wheel. She was a very beautiful woman.

"Okay, lady, where's the fire?"

She looked at him for a long moment and replied: "In your eyes, officer. In your eyes."

He let her go.

A doctor and his wife were walking down the street. The doctor warmly greeted a beautiful girl on the far side of the street. She waved back and smiled.

"Do you know that woman?" demanded the doctor's wife.

"Only professionally, darling," said the doctor.

"Only professionally, eh. Whose, yours or hers?"

"I'd let those doctors experiment on me for the sake of science. I'm not afraid. I've gone through the war. Why I even once volunteered to let them put a new heart into my chest if one was available which suited my character."

"What's the matter, couldn't they find a chicken big enough?"

In a pea-soupy fog off the North Atlantic coast, a big steamship collided with a fishing trawler. Some slight damage occurred to the trawler, but as the liner tried to back away, it again bruised the fishing boat.

The captain of the steamship, now worried, flashed a message to the smaller vessel: "Can you stay afloat?"

Back came the reply: "Yes, why? Are you going to try again?"

Sometimes kids put you down and don't really mean to.

George Dolanin in his column in the *Fort Worth Star-Telegram* reported the true observation of one of cub scout master Jim Rosenthal's kids:

"I want to be just like you when I grow up, sir."

"That's very nice, Bobby, but why?"

"Because you're happy . . . even if you ARE poor and old."

Guy and girl on dance floor. He whispers: "I want to dance like this forever, darling."

She whispers in his ear: "You mean you don't want to improve?"

Gary Moore was a great putter-downer. As host of two very popular shows for years he got hundreds of crank letters. He answered them all this way:

Dear Sir:

I am enclosing a letter I received from some idiot crackpot who is obviously using your name without your knowledge. I thought you would want to know.

Sincerely,

Gary Moore

"Got anything on for tonight, honey?"

"Yes, and I'm keeping it on."

"You couldn't loan me ten bucks 'til payday, could you?"

"How did you know my answer?"

It's 10:30 P.M. The young man has delivered his date back to her front door after a big night on the town. A double-feature movie, a hamburger, and a coke.

205

She speaks: "I'd love to go out with you again, Harold . . . after they've increased the minimum wage law!"

Two call girls, not overly fond of each other, were talking about the previous night's activities.

Lulu said: "Hey, last night I was with a guy who said, because he was enjoying my company so much, that he was giving me five hundred dollars!"

"Five hundred dollars?" purred her friend. "Imagine that, a four hundred and ninety-five dollar tip!"

Is there a worse feeling, girls, than when your husband looks at you very hard and says: "I know about you and the TV repairman."

Some wipeouts are just plain mean, but the victim often deserves it. There is one American sales representative who practices a method of putdown that lingers for some time.

When an executive's secretary gives him the usual: "Mr. Green is not in at the moment, would you care to leave your name and phone number?"

"No, no, that's okay," he tells the girl. "Just tell him that the Bureau of Internal Revenue called and that we'll be back!"

That'll leave a guy worrying for awhile.

It isn't too often an adult gets the last word where teenagers are concerned. But it happens. Rarely, but it happens.

Two long-haired teeners in a souped-up hot rod pulled up alongside a man in an XKE.

"Race?" said the kids.

Our hero looked at the boys for a moment and then answered slowly, "Caucasian."

206

A Texan, in Paris on holiday, inundated everyone he met in the City of Lights with the charms and the advantages of being born in the mighty State of Texas. He must have really thrown himself into his enthusiasm, for one day in the middle of a speech about Texas in a Paris restaurant, he died of a heart attack; he was buried ten days later.

Some months later the undertaker who had been given the dubious honor of burying the big Texan was telling another visiting Texan about it. . . . Now understand, this undertaker was a nice guy, but Texan number two was almost as obnoxious as the original, so he decided to let him have it.

"I'll never forget it," said the undertaker. "That fella from Texas, he was a big man, must've been six feet seven. Weighed five hundred pounds. There wasn't a coffin in all of Paris that we could put that big man in. But finally my assistant, Pierre, he came up with the answer."

"What did y'all do?" asked the Texan.

"It was easy. We gave him an enema and buried him in a shoe box."

Like to put a guy down and not really be rude about it? When introduced to him, just look at him very hard and say: "Oh, yes . . . of course, I know you by reputation."

When you're sounding off about any special talent or ability, be wary. You never know who's listening.

At a golf club, a recent Vic Tanny graduate was boasting about his strength and went on about it for some time. The greens-keeper overheard and made him this offer:

"Tell you what, I'll bet you twenty-five dollars that I can wheel a load in this wheelbarrow over there to the first tee that you can't wheel back."

"You're on," said Mr. Motor-mouth. "What's your load going to be?"

"Get in," said the gardener.

How to flatten the uninvited party crasher . . . particularly a troublesome one.

A charming New York hostess at a party in her home, walked up to the unwelcome pest and smiled sweetly: "I hear you've been looking for me—to say goodnight!"

Artist: "What do you think I should get for this painting?"

Critic: "Six months."

Is it really possible to one-up a loan company? We know a chap who did it beautifully.

He received a letter from his friendly loan company that said in part: ". . . You have been delinquent for several payments now. An action will soon be taken. What would your neighbors think if we came out and seized your car and house and furniture?"

Our friend wrote back: "Dear Friendly Finance Company: I have taken up the question with my neighbors and they think it would be a pretty lousy trick!"

Another guy harassed by a loan company for being a little late simply wrote back: "Dear Friendly Loan Company: This will acknowledge your letter of the fourth instant. . . . Go forth and multiply."

The new village doctor, fresh from college, was seeing one of his first patients.

"Before you came to see me, who was treating you for this illness?" he asked.

"Just ol' man Watkins down the corner drugstore," answered his patient.

The doctor, unable to conceal his annoyance at an unqualified person dispensing medical advice, blurted out: "And just what kind of stupid advice did that incompetent old man give you?"

"He told me to come and see you."

Ladies, like to put down the old man? Easy . . . just five little words that'll get him home in a jiffy.

Next time he phones to say he'll be working late at the office, simply breathe into the telephone: "John, can I count on that?"

A lovely young thing on a Mediterranean cruise complained about everything: the food, the service, and the facilities. On the fifth day out, she said to the captain:

"Look, every day so far I've been seated at dinner with a bunch of women. I'm sure you could arrange it so I could dine with some young bachelors. I've been dying to meet some nice young men."

The captain said he would change the seating arrangements for the following day to accommodate her wishes.

Next day, when she came into the ship's dining room, she found the steward had seated her at a table with six young priests!

A drunk at the corner bar was boring all his drinking pals with long speeches about the world situation in general but the new morality in particular.

"S'awful," he slurred, "the way young people carry on nowadays with their pre-marital activities and their extra-marital activities. Take me, for example. I never had intercourse with my wife before I married her . . . did you?"

All was quiet for a moment 'til one of the boys quipped: "Can't say for sure, Charlie, what was her maiden name?"

The girls in the office had been suffering the bragging and strutting of their office manager for quite some time when he burst into the office one morning, puffed out his chest, and announced: "Hey, everybody! My wife is pregnant!"

"Yeah! Really?" asked a little steno at the back of the office. "And, whom do you suspect?"

Morey Amsterdam tells about the blowhard air force major who had just been promoted to colonel and got a brand-new office. Corner office, better view, broadloom . . . the works. His first morning behind the desk, an airman knocked on the door and asked to speak to him. The colonel, feeling the urge to impress the young airman, picked up his phone and said:

"Yes, General, thank you. . . . Yes, I will pass that along to the President this afternoon. Yes, good-bye, sir."

Then, turning to the airman he barked: "And what do you want?"

"Nothing important, sir," said the airman. "I just came to install your telephone."

It seems there was this surly politician who made life miserable for his speech writer. A politician's speech writer is a very important fellow. He does all the research, outlines all the pertinent facts, assembles all the sonorous phrases, and then turns a finished polished speech over to Mr. Big to read to his audience.

This particular pundit was impossible to satisfy. The speeches were never right. Either the writing was bad or the speeches were too long or too short. It seems there was always something wrong with the material. Finally, our fed-up friend, after completing a very important speech for his boss on America's foreign policy, decided to quit. He laid his plans carefully. He gave the speech to the politician minutes before he was to deliver it before Congress and left forever.

Although the speaker did have time to at least glance quickly through the speech, he didn't bother. Instead he went before his colleagues "cold." He orated down through several pages of type prepared by the ghostwriter 'til he came to a passage which he read with special forcefulness, just the way his former speech writer had prepared it. . . .

". . . And now, I give you the ten vital reasons why this country should immediately withdraw its armed forces from Viet Nam."

He turned the next page and read on, loudly and importantly. The words prepared for him were: "Okay, fathead, now you're on your own."

A police officer stopped a vehicle careening down the highway. It turned out to be a haughty matron behind the wheel who spewed forth a bilge of abuse the moment the officer approached her car.

"The trouble with you policemen," she screamed, "is that you spend all your time chasing innocent citizens. Why don't you catch some of those drunk drivers?"

"Lady," offered the policeman quietly, "I thought I had one."

An American in Zurich to new-found Swiss "friends":

"America? I'm proud to be an American. The United States is the most civilized Christian nation on Earth!"

"That may very well be true, m'sieu, but you still can't deliver a payroll without an armored car."

It is reported that Bobby Kennedy once asked his secretary to get him Senator Long on the phone. He then told Senator Long in the strongest terms that he regretted the senator's unfortunate and undeserved public criticisms about "my record in the Attorney General's office."

"I have never even discussed that subject with the papers," answered the irritated senator. "I think you are talking to the wrong Senator Long. This is Senator Long of Louisiana. You must mean the other Senator Long."

"Oh, I'm so sorry," apologized Kennedy. "You're the nice Long."

"That's right . . . and which Senator Kennedy are you?"

You won't believe this, but even Santa at Christmas time can be a loser at the hands of the tad-types.

One kid patiently waited his turn in line at the department store and kicked Santa in the shin—very hard.

"What's that for?" asked Mr. Claus.

"That's for last year, Santa."

"What would you like for Christmas, son?" asked Santa of the five-year-old lad.

"I want a train and a car, a gun, a tank, some soldiers, a bugle, some games, and a truck."

"Okay, son, you be a good boy, now run along."

"You better write it down, Santa, you'll forget."

"Don't worry, my boy, Santa won't forget. Just you be a good boy and run along."

The kid went to the end of the line, patiently worked his way up to the great man again and Santa greeted him with: "And what would *you* like for Christmas, m'boy?"

"See! See!" screamed the boy. "You've forgotten already!"

Boy, when even the government by the people, for the people puts you down, it's time to resign from the world, isn't it?

A poultry farmer was experiencing a bad winter. He

was losing a lot of his prize hens. He wrote to the Department of Agriculture:

Gentlemen:

I need help. A very mysterious thing is happening on my farm, that I really don't understand. Every morning when I go out to the coop several of my chickens are lying on their backs, all stiff and their feet in the air. Can you tell me what is the matter, sir?

Yours sincerely,

Abraham Vine

Back came the reply.

Dear Mr. Vine:

Your chickens are dead.

A middle-aged, well-dressed gentleman walked into a menswear store and was approached by a curvaceous, sensuous, lovely female clerk who purred:

"And what is your desire, sir?" Adding a little wiggle of the bait.

He sighed a long sigh and looked right at her and said: "My dear, my desire is to grab you, kiss you, hug you, caress and fondle you, sweep you up in my arms, and rush you over to my apartment where I would pour some drinks, play the stereo, and make passionate love to you. However, my *need* is a pair of socks. Size eleven, please."

A disgruntled vacationer, who was less than happy with his accommodation and service, was checking out of his hotel in Miami, when the clerk suggested:

"You might be interested in these picture postcards, sir. There are some excellent views of this hotel."

"Thanks anyway, buddy, I have my own views of this hotel."

A small merchant had been trying unsuccessfully for months to collect an overdue bill from a customer. He tried everything. Finally, as a last resort, he sent an impassioned letter and enclosed a picture of his baby daughter. Under the picture he wrote: "It is because of this little one that I must have the money."

Back came the reply with a photo of a lovely curvaceous blonde under which was written: "It is because of this little one that I can't pay."

Man and wife were sitting quietly at home one evening when, suddenly, she leaped to her feet, dashed over, and kicked him in the leg.

"What the heck was that for?" he asked.

"That's for being a lousy lover."

He immediately retaliated by kicking her rear.

"What was that for?" she demanded.

"For knowing the difference."

The credit department of a large northern trading company got a letter from one of their catalogue customers in the northwest territories which read:

"I got your letter about what I owe. You have to be pachant. I ain't forgot. When I got the money, then you'll get it. If this was the judgment day and you was no more ready to meet your maker than I am to meet your bill you sure would go to hell. Trusting you will do this."

Yours truly,

Abraham Jenkins

How to raise a brighter child

These new methods, based on the theories of famous physicians, educators and behavioral scientists, are simple and fun—and they can increase your child's I. Q. by 20 points or more! Start using them as early as possible—even right after birth!

Imagine a 21-month-old with a reading vocabulary of 160 words...a boy of four who enjoys teaching himself major number principles...a girl not yet four who reads at the third grade level! None of these children was born a genius. Yet, through the early learning concepts described in this remarkable new book—HOW TO RAISE A BRIGHTER CHILD—all are being helped to develop above-average intelligence and a joyous love of learning.

Now you can give your little pre-schooler the same happy advantages...and they may well last throughout your child's life. For according to recent research, a child's I. Q. level is not permanently fixed at birth. It can be raised—or lowered by 20 points or even more in the precious years before six, by the way you rear your child at home.

Take the book now for a 30-day FREE trial

Send now for your copy of HOW TO RAISE A BRIGHTER CHILD. When it arrives, turn to the section that applies to your child *right now*, at this particular stage in his life. Apply some of the early learning techniques it shows you how to use. Then if not convinced this one book can make a world of difference in your child's mental development, return it within 30 days and owe nothing. If you decide to keep the book, it is yours for only $5.95 plus a small mailing charge. Take advantage of this opportunity! See your bookseller or mail the coupon today.

Joan Beck is known by millions of readers who follow her syndicated column, "You And Your Child." A graduate of Northwestern University, holding Bachelor's and Master's degrees, she has received several academic and professional awards and honors. She is married to Ernest W. Beck, a medical illustrator. They have two children, aged 15 and 12.

HOW IT WORKS

From color camera to computer

1,071 two-color drawings

Easy-to-understand explanations

HOW IS color television transmitted? (See page 166 of THE WAY THINGS WORK.) How does a helicopter fly? (See page 560.) How does "dry cleaning" clean? (See page 407.)

THE WAY THINGS WORK is a lucid encyclopedia of technology, an endlessly fascinating anthology of descriptions and diagrams that unravel the mystery of common mechanisms and today's technological marvels. It's a book to delight everyone intrigued with the way things work.

We invite you to mail the coupon below. A copy of THE WAY THINGS WORK will be sent to you at once. If at the end of ten days you do not feel that this book is one you will treasure, you may return it and owe nothing. Otherwise, we will bill you $8.95, plus postage and handling. At all bookstores, or write to Simon & Schuster, Inc., Dept. W-3, 630 Fifth Ave., New York, N.Y. 10020.

SIMON & SCHUSTER, Inc., Dept. W-3
630 Fifth Ave., New York, N. Y. 10020

Please send me .... copies of THE WAY THINGS WORK. If after examining it for 10 days, I am not completely delighted, I may return the book and owe nothing. Otherwise, you will bill me for $8.95 plus mailing costs.

Name ....

Address..

City........................... State............... Zip..........

☐ **SAVE!** Enclose $8.95 now and we pay postage. Same 10-day privilege with full refund guaranteed. (Please add applicable sales tax.)
